I0007734

Table of contents

Introduction

Chapter 3: Getting Started: Initial Setup and Navigation

Chapter 4: Essential Practical Skills for Beginners

Chapter 5: Integrating with AI via MCP

Chapter 6: Basic Troubleshooting and Maintenance

6.1 Identifying and Resolving Common Beginner Issues

6.2 Simple Monitoring and Health Checks

6.3 Essential Maintenance Practices for Beginners

6.4 Basic Security Tips for New Users

Chapter 7: Further Learning and Next Steps

7.1 Where to Find Additional Resources and Support

7.2 Suggestions for Continued Learning and Skill Development

7.3 Exploring More Advanced MCP Server Concepts

Introduction: Welcome to Your MCP Server Journey

If you've picked up this book, you're likely curious about something called an "MCP Server." Maybe you've heard it mentioned in tech circles, perhaps you're looking to streamline some processes, or maybe you're just eager to explore a new area of technology. Whatever your reason, you've come to the right place. Think of this book as your friendly guide, your personal sherpa, leading you through the often-perplexing landscape of MCP servers.

Now, I know "server" can sound intimidating. Images of blinking lights in a cold, dark room might pop into your head. But trust me, while MCP servers can be powerful and sophisticated, the core concepts are surprisingly accessible, especially when we break them down step by step – which is exactly what we're going to do.

In my own journey through the tech world, I've often found that the biggest hurdle isn't the complexity of the technology itself, but the way it's explained. That's why this book is designed to be different. We're going to skip the heavy jargon and focus on clear, straightforward language. We'll use analogies to make abstract ideas more concrete, and we'll emphasize practical applications so you can see the real-world value of what you're learning.

Think of an MCP server a bit like a central hub or a very efficient assistant. It's designed to manage and coordinate various tasks and resources, often in a way that makes things simpler and more organized for you or for other systems. The "MCP" part, which we'll delve into more deeply later, adds a layer of intelligence and connectivity, especially when it comes to interacting with the exciting world of Artificial Intelligence.

Over the years, I've seen firsthand how powerful these kinds of centralized systems can be. They can automate repetitive tasks, provide a single point of control for complex operations, and even unlock new possibilities by connecting different tools and data in intelligent ways. And while the term "MCP server" might be new to you now, by the end of this book, you'll have a solid understanding of what it is, how it works, and how you can start to leverage its potential.

This book is structured to take you on a logical learning journey. We'll start with the fundamental concepts, building a strong foundation before moving on to practical skills. You'll learn about the key components of an MCP server, how to potentially set one up (if applicable to the specific type we're focusing on), how to navigate its interface, and most importantly, how to use its core functionalities to achieve real results.

We'll also touch upon the exciting integration of MCP servers with Artificial Intelligence through the Model Context Protocol (MCP). This is a rapidly evolving area, and understanding the basics here will give you a significant head start in comprehending the future of intelligent systems.

Don't worry if you're a complete beginner. This book assumes no prior knowledge. We'll take things at a comfortable pace, and I'll be right here with you every step of the way. My goal is not just to inform you, but to empower you to confidently explore and utilize MCP server technology.

So, buckle up! You're about to embark on an exciting journey into the world of MCP servers. By the time you turn the last page, you'll have a practical understanding and the foundational skills to start applying this knowledge in your own endeavors. Let's get started

Chapter 1: Understanding the Basics of MCP Server

In this first chapter, we're going to lay the groundwork by answering the most fundamental question: What exactly *is* an MCP server? Don't worry, we'll break it down into bite-sized pieces and use some relatable analogies to make it crystal clear.

1.1 What is an MCP Server? Unpacking the Central Coordinator

In our initial foray, we likened an MCP server to an efficient office manager. While that analogy serves as a helpful entry point, the reality is richer and more nuanced. Think of an MCP server not just as a coordinator, but as a **dynamic, intelligent orchestration engine** within a digital ecosystem.

At its core, an MCP server is a software framework or platform designed to **centralize the management, access, and interaction with a diverse range of digital resources and capabilities.** These resources can span from traditional data repositories (databases, file systems) and application programming interfaces (APIs) to more contemporary elements like specialized tools and, crucially, Artificial Intelligence models.

The "server" aspect denotes its role as a provider of services. It listens for requests from various "clients" – which can be applications, other systems, or even AI agents – and responds by facilitating access to the managed resources or executing specific functions.

However, the "MCP" – Model Context Protocol – distinguishes it from a generic server. This protocol imbues the server with an understanding of how AI models operate and the specific ways they need to interact with external resources. It's not just about connecting systems; it's about **intelligently mediating the relationship between AI and the broader digital landscape.**

Consider a symphony orchestra. Each musician (analogous to a digital resource or AI model) is highly skilled but needs a conductor (the MCP server) to bring harmony and coherence to their performance. The conductor understands the capabilities of each instrument and guides their interplay to create a unified and meaningful output. The "score" they follow, in a sense, is the Model Context Protocol – a set of rules and guidelines that ensure everyone is playing from the same sheet.

The Purpose: Enabling Intelligent Interaction and Streamlined Operations

The fundamental purpose of an MCP server is two-fold:

1. **To empower AI models with seamless and contextual access to external resources:** Traditional methods of integrating AI often involve complex, bespoke connections and data transformations. MCP provides a standardized

and efficient pathway for AI to retrieve information, utilize tools, and interact with the real world in a more natural and intuitive way. This reduces the "friction" in AI application development and deployment.

- *Personal Insight:* I've witnessed the frustration of trying to connect different AI models to disparate data silos. The lack of a common language often leads to brittle and time-consuming integrations. MCP offers a much-needed paradigm shift towards interoperability.

2. **To streamline and centralize the management of diverse digital assets:** Beyond its AI-centric role, an MCP server offers significant advantages in terms of organizing and controlling a variety of digital resources. By providing a single point of access and management, it simplifies governance, enhances security, and improves overall operational efficiency.

In essence, an MCP server aims to create a more **cohesive and intelligent digital environment** where AI can be a more deeply integrated and effective component. It moves beyond simple data pipelines to establish a dynamic and context-aware interaction layer.

1.2 Core Terminology Explained (Nodes, Services, Protocols, Client/Server, MCP)

Alright, let's dissect the essential vocabulary that forms the bedrock of understanding MCP servers. These terms are the fundamental building blocks, and grasping them firmly will make your journey through the intricacies of MCP much smoother. While providing complete, working, and up-to-date code examples for each term in isolation can be challenging without a specific MCP server implementation in mind, I can illustrate their practical relevance with conceptual code snippets and analogies.

Think of this section as your personal glossary for navigating the world of MCP servers. We'll break down each key term, explore its significance, and connect it to real-world scenarios.

Nodes: The Individual Actors

In the context of an MCP server, **nodes** represent the individual entities or components that the server manages or interacts with. These can be physical servers, virtual machines, software applications, specific functions within a system, or even individual AI models themselves. The MCP server orchestrates and coordinates the activities of these diverse nodes.

- **Significance:** Understanding nodes is crucial for grasping the distributed nature of many MCP server deployments. Tasks and resources are often spread across multiple nodes for scalability, resilience, and efficiency.[1]

- **Analogy:** Imagine a team of specialists in our office. Each specialist (node) has a particular skill set (service they provide). The MCP server manages how these specialists collaborate on projects.

- **Conceptual Code Snippet (Illustrative - Python):**

- Python

```python
class Node:

    def __init__(self, node_id, capabilities):

        self.node_id = node_id

        self.capabilities = capabilities


    def execute_task(self, task):

        if task in self.capabilities:

            print(f"Node {self.node_id} executing task: {task}")

            return True

        else:

            print(f"Node {self.node_id} cannot execute task: {task}")
```

```
        return False


node1 = Node("data_processor_01", ["data_analysis",
"data_storage"])

node2 = Node("ai_model_05", ["text_generation",
"sentiment_analysis"])



node1.execute_task("data_analysis")  # Output: Node
data_processor_01 executing task: data_analysis

node2.execute_task("image_recognition") # Output: Node
ai_model_05 cannot execute task: image_recognition
```

Services: The Offered Capabilities

Services are the specific functionalities or capabilities that the nodes within the MCP server ecosystem provide or that the MCP server itself manages and exposes. These can range from data access and manipulation to the execution of specific algorithms or the invocation of external APIs.

- **Significance:** Services are the practical value proposition of the MCP server. They represent the concrete actions that clients (including AI) can request and utilize.

- **Analogy:** Back to our office, services are like the specific departments: IT support (provides technical assistance), HR (manages personnel), Sales (handles customer interactions).

- **Conceptual Code Snippet (Illustrative - Python):**

- Python

```python
class DataService:

    def get_data(self, query):

        print(f"Fetching data based on query: {query}")

        return {"results": [...] }


class AiService:

    def analyze_sentiment(self, text):

        print(f"Analyzing sentiment of text: '{text}'")

        return "Positive"


data_service = DataService()

ai_service = AiService()
```

```
data = data_service.get_data("SELECT * FROM customers
WHERE region='Onitsha'")

sentiment = ai_service.analyze_sentiment("The service was
excellent!")

print(f"Data: {data}")

print(f"Sentiment: {sentiment}")
```

Protocols: The Language of Communication

Protocols are the sets of rules and procedures that govern how different components within the MCP server ecosystem communicate with each other. They define the format of messages, the sequence of interactions, and the error handling mechanisms.

- **Significance:** Standardized protocols ensure interoperability and reliable communication between diverse systems and AI models.[2] The MCP itself is a key protocol in this context.

- **Analogy:** Protocols are like the agreed-upon languages spoken in our office. Everyone needs to understand the same language to collaborate effectively. HTTP, TCP/IP, and MCP are examples of such languages in the digital realm.

- **Conceptual Code Snippet (Illustrative - Python - focusing on a simplified request/response):**

- Python

```python
def send_request(protocol, destination, message):

    print(f"Sending message '{message}' to {destination} using {protocol}")

    # Simulate sending over the network

    response = receive_response(protocol, destination)

    return response


def receive_response(protocol, source):

    print(f"Receiving response from {source} using {protocol}")

    return {"status": "success", "data": "Processed"}


response = send_request("MCP", "ai_model_05", {"action": "analyze", "text": "Hello"})

print(f"Response received: {response}")
```

Client/Server: The Request-Response Dynamic

The **client/server** model is a fundamental architectural pattern where a **client** (e.g., an application, an AI agent) makes a request for a service or resource to a **server** (in this case, the MCP server or a node managed by it), and the server responds to that request.

- **Significance:** This model underpins most interactions within an MCP server environment, enabling on-demand access to services and data.

- **Analogy:** In our office, an employee (client) might request IT support (server) for a technical issue. The IT department receives the request and provides a solution.

- **Conceptual Code Snippet (Illustrative - Python - a very basic client):**

- Python

```python
class McpClient:

  def __init__(self, server_address):

    self.server_address = server_address
```

```python
def request_service(self, service_name, parameters):

    print(f"Client sending request to {self.server_address} for
service '{service_name}' with parameters: {parameters}")

    # Simulate sending a request over the network

    response = self._simulate_server_response(service_name,
parameters)

    return response


def _simulate_server_response(self, service_name,
parameters):

    if service_name == "get_user_data":

        user_id = parameters.get("user_id")

        if user_id:

            return {"status": "success", "data": {"user_id": user_id,
"name": "Example User", "location": "Onitsha"}}

        else:

            return {"status": "error", "message": "Missing user_id"}

    return {"status": "unknown"}
```

```
client = McpClient("mcp_server:8080")

user_data = client.request_service("get_user_data", {"user_id":
"123"})

print(f"Client received: {user_data}")
```

MCP (Model Context Protocol): The AI Interaction Standard

The **Model Context Protocol (MCP)** is the linchpin that enables intelligent interaction between AI models and the resources managed by the MCP server. It's a standardized set of rules and specifications that define how AI models can request and receive information, utilize tools, and interact with the broader digital environment in a context-aware manner.

- **Significance:** MCP is crucial for unlocking the full potential of AI within an MCP server ecosystem. It fosters interoperability, simplifies development, and enhances the ability of AI to reason and act based on relevant context.

- **Analogy:** MCP is like a specialized language and set of procedures designed specifically for our intelligent intern (AI model) to effectively communicate with and utilize the resources of the office (MCP server). It ensures the intern asks for things in a way the office understands and receives information in a usable format.

- **Conceptual Code Snippet (Illustrative - Python - focusing on a simplified MCP request structure):**

- Python

```python
mcp_request = {

    "model_id": "text-davinci-003",

    "action": "generate_summary",

    "context": {

        "document_id": "report_2023.pdf",

        "user_query": "Summarize the key findings."

    },

    "response_format": "text"

}


def process_mcp_request(request):

    model_id = request.get("model_id")

    action = request.get("action")

    context = request.get("context")
```

```python
    # Simulate processing based on the MCP request

    if action == "generate_summary" and "document_id" in context:

        document_id = context["document_id"]

        # ... logic to retrieve and summarize the document ...

        summary = f"Summary of {document_id}: ..."

        return {"status": "success", "result": summary}

    else:

        return {"status": "error", "message": "Invalid MCP request"}


mcp_response = process_mcp_request(mcp_request)

print(f"MCP Response: {mcp_response}")
```

1.3 Benefits for Beginners and Common Use Cases

As a beginner, you might be wondering, "Why should I invest time in understanding MCP servers?" The answer lies in the tangible benefits they offer, even at an introductory level, and the increasingly relevant use cases they enable, particularly in the evolving landscape of AI.

Benefits for Beginners: Simplifying Complexity

While the underlying technology can be sophisticated, the *concept* of an MCP server offers several advantages that can be particularly helpful for those new to managing digital resources and exploring AI integration:

- **Centralized Organization:** Instead of dealing with disparate systems and scattered data, an MCP server provides a unified platform. This central view simplifies the mental model required to understand and interact with various resources. Think of it as having all your important apps organized on a single dashboard instead of scattered across multiple screens.

    - *Conceptual Illustration:* Imagine trying to access customer data, analytics tools, and AI models through three different logins and interfaces. An MCP server aims to integrate these under a single umbrella.
- **Simplified AI Integration:** For beginners venturing into AI, the MCP offers a more structured and less intimidating way to connect AI models with data and tools. Instead of grappling with low-level API calls and custom data pipelines, the MCP provides a standardized communication layer.

- *Personal Insight:* My early experiences with AI integration often felt like navigating a maze of different API specifications and authentication methods. MCP promises a more streamlined and consistent approach, which would have been a huge boon for my initial learning curve.

- **Abstraction of Complexity:** The MCP server handles much of the intricate communication and data handling behind the scenes. This allows beginners to focus on the *what* they want to achieve (e.g., analyze customer sentiment) rather than the *how* of connecting the AI model to the relevant data.

  - *Conceptual Illustration:* Instead of writing complex code to fetch data, format it, and send it to an AI model, an MCP client might offer a simpler function call:

    ```
    mcp_client.analyze_data(data_source="cu
    stomer_reviews",
    analysis_type="sentiment").
    ```

- **Learning a Future-Relevant Skill:** As AI continues to permeate various industries, understanding how AI interacts with underlying infrastructure becomes increasingly valuable. Learning about MCP servers now equips you with a foundational understanding of this critical aspect.

Common Use Cases: Real-World Applications

To make the benefits more concrete, let's explore some common use cases where MCP servers are proving their worth, even in scenarios relevant to beginners or those exploring introductory applications:

- **Simplified Data Access for AI Assistants:** Imagine building a basic AI chatbot that needs to answer user questions based on a knowledge base. An MCP server can manage the connection to this knowledge base (e.g., a collection of documents or a FAQ database). The AI chatbot, using MCP, can then easily query the server for relevant information without needing to know the specifics of the database structure or access methods.

  - *Conceptual Workflow:* User asks chatbot -> Chatbot (MCP Client) sends MCP request to MCP Server -> MCP Server retrieves information from knowledge base -> MCP Server sends MCP response to Chatbot -> Chatbot answers user.

- **Orchestrating Basic Automation with AI:** Consider a scenario where you want to automate the process of summarizing customer feedback. An MCP server can manage access to the customer feedback data and also host or connect to an AI model capable of text summarization. A simple automated workflow, potentially triggered through the MCP server, could involve fetching new feedback, sending it to the AI model via MCP for summarization, and then storing the summaries.

- *Conceptual Code Snippet (Illustrative - Python - simplified automation):*

- Python

```python
def summarize_feedback(mcp_client):

    new_feedback = get_new_customer_feedback() # Assume this function retrieves new data

    if new_feedback:

        mcp_request = {

            "model_id": "text-summarizer-v1",

            "action": "summarize",

            "context": {"text": new_feedback},

            "response_format": "text"

        }

        response = mcp_client.send_mcp_request(mcp_request)

        if response and response.get("status") == "success":
```

```
        store_summary(response["result"]) # Assume this function
stores the summary

        print("Feedback summarized successfully.")

    else:

        print("Error during summarization.")

    else:

    print("No new feedback to summarize.")


# Assuming 'mcp_client' is an initialized MCP client object

# summarize_feedback(mcp_client)
```

- ○
- **Integrating AI with Simple Tools:** Imagine an AI agent that needs to schedule a meeting. An MCP server could provide access to a calendar API.[8] The AI, using MCP, can request the server to check availability and book appointments without needing to directly interact with the complexities of the calendar API.[9]

    - ○ *Conceptual Interaction:* AI Agent (MCP Client) -> MCP Request ("check_availability", parameters) -> MCP Server -> Calendar API -> MCP Response (available slots) -> AI Agent -> MCP Request ("book_appointment", parameters) -> MCP Server -> Calendar API.

- **Learning Platform for AI Interaction:** For beginners learning about AI, an MCP server can provide a controlled and structured environment to experiment with how AI models interact with data and tools. It can abstract away some of the underlying complexities, allowing learners to focus on the core concepts of AI interaction.

  - *Personal Reflection:* I often wished for a more sandbox-like environment when first learning about AI integration. An MCP server can potentially serve this purpose, offering a more guided and less error-prone way to explore these interactions.

While these examples are simplified, they illustrate the potential of MCP servers to make AI integration more accessible and to streamline the management of digital resources, even for those just starting their journey. As you progress, you'll discover even more sophisticated and powerful use cases. The key takeaway is that MCP servers aim to make the intelligent digital world more manageable and accessible to everyone.

1.4 The Role of Model Context Protocol (MCP) Explained Simply: The AI's Universal Translator

Imagine you're an incredibly intelligent being (an AI model) who has just landed on a new planet (our digital world managed by an MCP server). This planet is full of valuable resources (data, tools, functionalities), but everyone speaks different languages and has their own unique way of doing things. Without a universal translator and a set of common interaction rules, navigating this world and utilizing its resources would be incredibly difficult and inefficient.

This, in essence, is the problem that the Model Context Protocol (MCP) aims to solve. It acts as that **universal translator and set of interaction rules**, specifically designed for AI models to communicate effectively with MCP servers and the diverse ecosystem they manage.

Core Principles of MCP:

1. **Standardized Request Format:** MCP defines a consistent structure for how AI models can request information or actions from an MCP server. This standardization ensures that the server can understand requests from various AI models, regardless of their underlying architecture or training.

- Conceptual Illustration (JSON-like):

- JSON

```json
{

 "model_id": "my_cool_llm_v2",

 "action": "retrieve_data",

 "context": {

  "data_source": "customer_database",

  "query": "SELECT * FROM orders WHERE date > '2024-01-01' AND product = 'widget'"

 },

 "response_format": "json"

}
```

- **Explanation:** This request clearly specifies the AI model making the request (`model_id`), the desired action (`retrieve_data`), the relevant context (which data source and the specific query), and the preferred format for the response (`json`).

2. **Contextual Awareness:** The "Context" element within MCP is crucial. It allows AI models to provide specific

33

details about what they need and why. This context enables the MCP server to understand the intent behind the request and provide more relevant and accurate responses.

- *Personal Insight:* The lack of rich contextual information has often been a bottleneck in AI interactions. MCP's emphasis on context allows for more nuanced and intelligent exchanges.

3. **Capability Discovery:** Ideally, MCP facilitates a way for AI models to discover the available services and data sources managed by the MCP server. This allows AI to dynamically adapt and utilize the resources at its disposal without needing prior, hardcoded knowledge.

- *Conceptual Interaction:* An AI model might send an MCP request like:

- JSON

```json
{

 "model_id": "smart_agent_alpha",

 "action": "discover_capabilities",

 "context": {"task": "analyze customer feedback"}

}
```

- The MCP server could then respond with a list of relevant services (e.g., "sentiment analysis," "topic extraction") and data sources (e.g., "customer reviews database").

4. **Standardized Response Format:** Just as requests are standardized, MCP also defines a consistent structure for how the MCP server returns information or the results of actions to the AI model.[7] This ensures that the AI can easily parse and utilize the response.

- *Conceptual Illustration (JSON-like response to the data retrieval request):*

- JSON

```
{

  "status": "success",

  "data": [

    {"order_id": 101, "product": "widget", "customer_id": 5},

    {"order_id": 102, "product": "widget", "customer_id": 12}

    // ... more order data ...

  ]
```

```
    }

        o
```

The MCP Server as the Intermediary:

The MCP server acts as the intelligent intermediary that
understands and enforces the MCP.[8] When an AI model sends an
MCP request:

1. **The server receives and parses the request.**
2. **It authenticates and authorizes the AI model** to ensure it
   has the necessary permissions to access the requested
   resources or perform the desired actions.
3. **It interprets the context of the request** to understand
   exactly what the AI needs.
4. **It interacts with the underlying data sources, tools, or
   services** to fulfill the request.
5. **It formats the response according to the MCP
   specifications** and sends it back to the AI model.

Why is MCP Crucial for AI Integration?

- **Interoperability:** MCP fosters seamless interaction
  between diverse AI models and a wide range of backend
  systems without the need for custom, point-to-point
  integrations.[9]
- **Efficiency:** Standardized communication reduces the
  complexity of development and deployment for AI-powered
  applications.

- **Contextual Relevance:** The emphasis on context ensures that AI models receive the precise information they need, leading to more accurate and effective outcomes.[10]
- **Scalability:** By providing a consistent interaction layer, MCP facilitates the development of more scalable and maintainable AI systems.[11]
- **Security:** The MCP server can enforce security policies and control access to sensitive resources, ensuring that AI interactions are secure and authorized.[12]

Conceptual Code Snippet (Illustrative - Python - a simplified MCP server interaction):

Python

```
# Assume a simplified MCP client library

class SimpleMcpClient:

  def __init__(self, server_address):

    self.server_address = server_address


  def send_mcp_request(self, request):

    print(f"Sending MCP request to {self.server_address}: {request}")

    # Simulate sending over network and receiving response
```

```python
        response = self._simulate_mcp_server_response(request)

        return response

    def _simulate_mcp_server_response(self, request):

        action = request.get("action")

        context = request.get("context")



        if action == "retrieve_data" and context.get("data_source") ==
"customer_database":

            query = context.get("query")

            if "widget" in query:

                return {"status": "success", "data": [{"product": "widget",
"customer_id": 5}, {"product": "widget", "customer_id": 12}]}

            else:

                return {"status": "success", "data": []}

        elif action == "discover_capabilities" and context.get("task")
== "analyze customer feedback":
```

```python
        return {"status": "success", "capabilities":
["sentiment_analysis", "topic_extraction"], "data_sources":
["customer_reviews_db"]}

    else:

        return {"status": "error", "message": "Invalid request or
unauthorized"}


# Example AI model interacting through the MCP client

mcp_client = SimpleMcpClient("mcp_server:8080")


# Requesting data

data_request = {

    "model_id": "my_analyzer_bot",

    "action": "retrieve_data",

    "context": {"data_source": "customer_database", "query":
"SELECT * FROM orders WHERE product = 'widget'"},

    "response_format": "json"

}

data_response = mcp_client.send_mcp_request(data_request)
```

```python
print(f"Data Response: {data_response}")


# Discovering capabilities

discovery_request = {

    "model_id": "smart_planner_ai",

    "action": "discover_capabilities",

    "context": {"task": "analyze customer feedback"}

}

discovery_response =
mcp_client.send_mcp_request(discovery_request)

print(f"Discovery Response: {discovery_response}")
```

While this code is a highly simplified illustration, it conveys the fundamental idea of an AI model (acting through an MCP client) sending structured requests to an MCP server and receiving standardized responses.

In conclusion, the Model Context Protocol (MCP) is the vital communication bridge that enables intelligent and efficient interaction between AI models and the rich resources managed by an MCP server. Its standardization, emphasis on context, and facilitation of capability discovery are key to unlocking the full potential of AI within a connected digital world. As AI continues to evolve, understanding and leveraging MCP will become increasingly crucial for building intelligent and integrated systems.

Chapter 2: MCP Server Architecture and Key Concepts

In the previous chapter, we established that an MCP server acts as a central coordinator. Now, let's explore the typical components that make up this coordinator and how they interact. Understanding this high-level architecture will give you a better grasp of how an MCP server functions and how its various parts work together.

2.1 High-Level Architecture Overview: The Blueprint of an Intelligent Hub

Think of the MCP server architecture as the blueprint of our intelligent office manager. It outlines the different departments and how they communicate to ensure smooth and efficient operations. While specific implementations can vary, a typical MCP server comprises several key components that work in concert:

1. The MCP Gateway/API Server: This is the entry point for all incoming requests, primarily from MCP clients (often AI models). It acts as the front desk, receiving requests, authenticating clients, and routing them to the appropriate internal components. It also handles the formatting of responses back to the clients according to the MCP specification.

- **Role:** Request reception, authentication, authorization, request routing, response formatting (MCP).

- **Analogy:** The friendly receptionist who greets visitors, verifies their credentials, and directs them to the right department.

- **Conceptual Code Snippet (Python - Flask-based micro-service):**

- Python

```python
from flask import Flask, request, jsonify

import uuid  # For simulating authentication


app = Flask(__name__)

AUTHORIZED_MODELS = {"model_alpha": "secret_key_alpha"}


def authenticate(model_id, api_key):

    return model_id in AUTHORIZED_MODELS and
AUTHORIZED_MODELS[model_id] == api_key
```

```python
@app.route('/mcp', methods=['POST'])

def handle_mcp_request():

    data = request.get_json()

    model_id = data.get('model_id')

    api_key = data.get('api_key') # Hypothetical authentication


    if not authenticate(model_id, api_key):

        return jsonify({"status": "error", "message": "Unauthorized"}),


    action = data.get('action')

    context = data.get('context')


    # In a real system, this would route to other components

    if action == 'retrieve_data' and context.get('data_source') ==
'example_db':

        query = context.get('query')

        results = simulate_data_retrieval(query)

        return jsonify({"status": "success", "data": results})
```

```python
    elif action == 'execute_tool' and context.get('tool_name') ==
'calculator':

        expression = context.get('expression')

        result = simulate_calculation(expression)

        return jsonify({"status": "success", "result": result})

    else:

        return jsonify({"status": "error", "message": "Invalid action or
context"})


def simulate_data_retrieval(query):

    print(f"Simulating data retrieval for query: {query}")

    return [{"id": 1, "value": "example"}, {"id": 2, "value": "another"}]


def simulate_calculation(expression):

    try:

        return eval(expression) # Be extremely cautious with eval in
production!

    except Exception as e:
```

```
    return f"Error: {e}"



if __name__ == '__main__':

    app.run(debug=True, port=5000)
```

-   ○ **Explanation:** This simplified Flask application acts
      as the MCP gateway. It receives POST requests at
      the `/mcp` endpoint, performs basic authentication,
      and then simulates routing the request based on the
      `action` and `context` to internal "services." In a real
      MCP server, these would be separate components.

2. Service Orchestration Layer: This component acts as the
brain of the MCP server. It receives processed requests from the
gateway and determines which internal services or external
resources are needed to fulfill them. It manages the flow of data
and control between different components.

-   **Role:** Request processing, service discovery, workflow
    management, data transformation (if needed).

-   **Analogy:** The central manager who receives instructions
    from the receptionist, understands which departments need
    to be involved, and coordinates their efforts.

- **Conceptual Code Snippet (Python - a simplified orchestrator class):**

- Python

```python
class ServiceOrchestrator:

    def __init__(self, data_service, tool_service):

        self.data_service = data_service

        self.tool_service = tool_service


    def process_request(self, action, context):

        if action == 'retrieve_data' and context.get('data_source') == 'example_db':

            query = context.get('query')

            return self.data_service.get_data(query)

        elif action == 'execute_tool' and context.get('tool_name') == 'calculator':

            expression = context.get('expression')

            return self.tool_service.calculate(expression)

        else:
```

```python
        return {"status": "error", "message": "Cannot process
request"}


class DataService:

    def get_data(self, query):

        print(f"Data Service: Retrieving data for '{query}'")

        return [{"id": 1, "value": "example"}, {"id": 2, "value":
"another"}]


class ToolService:

    def calculate(self, expression):

        try:

            return eval(expression)

        except Exception as e:

            return f"Tool Service Error: {e}"


# In a real system, these services would be more complex and
potentially running on different nodes
```

```
data_svc = DataService()

tool_svc = ToolService()

orchestrator = ServiceOrchestrator(data_svc, tool_svc)


result = orchestrator.process_request('retrieve_data',
{'data_source': 'example_db', 'query': 'SELECT *'})

print(f"Orchestrator Result (Data): {result}")


result = orchestrator.process_request('execute_tool', {'tool_name':
'calculator', 'expression': '2 + 2'})

print(f"Orchestrator Result (Tool): {result}")
```

-
    - **Explanation:** This shows a simplified
      `ServiceOrchestrator` that takes an action and
      context and then delegates the actual work to
      specific services (`DataService`, `ToolService`). In
      a real MCP server, the orchestrator would handle
      service discovery (finding the right service to call)
      and potentially more complex workflows.

3. Resource Connectors/Adapters: These components are
responsible for interacting with the actual backend resources, such

as databases, APIs of external tools, file systems, and even specific AI model inference endpoints. They abstract away the specific details of how to communicate with each type of resource, providing a consistent interface to the service orchestration layer.

- **Role:** Connecting to and interacting with backend resources, data translation, protocol adaptation.
- **Analogy:** Specialized liaisons who know how to communicate with different departments or external partners, regardless of their internal processes.
- **Conceptual Illustration:** A dedicated connector for a PostgreSQL database would handle the specific SQL dialect and connection protocols required to interact with it. Similarly, an adapter for a REST API would handle HTTP requests and response parsing.

4. Data Management Layer: This component handles the storage, retrieval, and potentially the caching of data used by the MCP server and the AI models it serves. It ensures efficient access to information.

- **Role:** Data storage, data retrieval, caching, data indexing.
- **Analogy:** The central filing system and archives of the office, ensuring information is organized and readily accessible.

5. Security and Access Control: This is a critical cross-cutting component that enforces authentication (verifying identity) and authorization (determining what actions are permitted) for all requests and interactions within the MCP server ecosystem.

- **Role:** Authentication, authorization, auditing, encryption.
- **Analogy:** The security guards and access control systems of the office, ensuring only authorized personnel can access specific areas and resources.

6. Monitoring and Logging: This component tracks the activity and performance of the MCP server and its managed resources. Logs provide valuable insights for debugging, auditing, and understanding system behavior.

- **Role:** Activity tracking, performance monitoring, error logging.
- **Analogy:** The security cameras and activity logs that record everything happening in the office, useful for review and identifying issues.

Interaction Flow:

A typical interaction flow for an AI model making a request to an MCP server would look something like this:

1. The AI model (acting as an MCP client) sends an MCP-formatted request to the **MCP Gateway/API Server**.
2. The **Gateway** authenticates and authorizes the AI model.
3. The **Gateway** forwards the request to the **Service Orchestration Layer**.

4. The **Orchestration Layer** determines which **Resource Connectors** are needed to fulfill the request.
5. The **Resource Connectors** interact with the appropriate backend resources (e.g., databases, APIs).
6. Data is retrieved and passed back through the **Connectors** to the **Orchestration Layer**.
7. The **Orchestration Layer** may perform some processing or aggregation of the data.
8. The **Orchestration Layer** formats the response according to the MCP specification.
9. The **Gateway** sends the MCP-formatted response back to the AI model.
10. Throughout this process, the **Security and Access Control** component ensures all interactions are authorized, and the **Monitoring and Logging** component tracks all activity.

2.2 Fundamental Concepts: Data, Resources, Security Basics

Think of these concepts as the foundational principles that guide how our intelligent office manager handles information, manages its assets, and ensures a safe and trustworthy environment.

Data: The Lifeblood of Intelligence

At its core, an MCP server is often concerned with managing and providing access to **data**. This data can take various forms, from structured databases and semi-structured documents to unstructured text and multimedia files. The MCP server acts as a central point for AI models and other applications to discover, retrieve, and potentially manipulate this data, all within defined access controls.

- **Significance:** Data is the fuel that powers AI. Without access to relevant and well-managed data, AI models cannot learn, reason, or perform effectively. The MCP server plays a vital role in making this data accessible in a contextually relevant way.

- **Conceptual Illustration:** Imagine an AI model tasked with generating product recommendations. The MCP server would provide it with access to customer purchase history data, product catalog information, and potentially even customer reviews.

- **Conceptual Code Snippet (Python - simulating data retrieval):**

- Python

```python
class DataManager:

    def __init__(self, data_sources):

        self.data_sources = data_sources
```

```python
    def retrieve(self, data_source_name, query):
        if data_source_name in self.data_sources:
            print(f"DataManager: Retrieving data from
'{data_source_name}' with query: '{query}'")
            # Simulate database query
            if data_source_name == "customer_database" and
"product = 'widget'" in query:
                return [{"customer_id": 1, "name": "Alice"},
{"customer_id": 5, "name": "Bob"}]
            else:
                return []
        else:
            return {"error": f"Data source '{data_source_name}'
not found."}


data_stores = {"customer_database": {...},
"product_catalog": {...}} # Simulate data sources

data_manager = DataManager(data_stores)
```

```
customer_data =
data_manager.retrieve("customer_database", "SELECT *
FROM customers WHERE product = 'widget'")
```

print(f"Retrieved Customer Data: {customer_data}")

- ○ **Explanation:** This simplified `DataManager`
  simulates how an MCP server might manage access
  to different data sources and retrieve data based on
  a query provided in the MCP request.

Resources: The Assets to be Managed

Beyond data, an MCP server also manages various **resources**.
These can include computational resources (CPU, GPU), network
bandwidth, access to external APIs and tools, and even the AI
models themselves (in scenarios where the MCP server
orchestrates multiple AI agents). Efficient management of these
resources is crucial for the performance and scalability of the
entire system.

- **Significance:** Proper resource allocation ensures that AI
  models and other services have the necessary capacity to
  operate effectively without bottlenecks or conflicts.

- **Conceptual Illustration:** If multiple AI models need to
  perform intensive computations, the MCP server might
  manage the allocation of GPU resources to ensure fair and

efficient utilization.

- **Conceptual Code Snippet (Python - simulating resource allocation):**

- Python

```python
class ResourceManager:

    def __init__(self, total_gpu_units=4):

        self.available_gpus = [True] * total_gpu_units


    def allocate_gpu(self):

        for i, available in enumerate(self.available_gpus):

            if available:

                self.available_gpus[i] = False

                print(f"ResourceManager: Allocated GPU unit {i}.")

                return i

        print("ResourceManager: No GPU units available.")
        return None
```

```python
def release_gpu(self, gpu_id):

    if 0 <= gpu_id < len(self.available_gpus) and not
self.available_gpus[gpu_id]:

        self.available_gpus[gpu_id] = True

        print(f"ResourceManager: Released GPU unit
{gpu_id}.")


resource_manager = ResourceManager()

gpu1 = resource_manager.allocate_gpu()

gpu2 = resource_manager.allocate_gpu()

resource_manager.release_gpu(gpu1)

gpu3 = resource_manager.allocate_gpu()
```

- ○ **Explanation:** This `ResourceManager` simulates
  the allocation and release of a limited number of
  GPU units, demonstrating a basic form of resource
  management within an MCP server context.

Security Basics: Ensuring Trust and Integrity

Security is a paramount concern for any system that manages sensitive data and facilitates interactions between different components, especially when AI models are involved. Fundamental security concepts within an MCP server context include:

- **Authentication:** Verifying the identity of clients (AI models, applications, users) trying to access the server. This ensures that only legitimate entities can interact with the system.

- **Authorization:** Determining what actions an authenticated client is permitted to perform and which resources it can access. This ensures that clients only have the necessary privileges.

- **Data Integrity:** Ensuring that data is accurate and has not been tampered with during storage or transmission.

- **Confidentiality:** Protecting sensitive data from unauthorized access. This often involves encryption both at rest and in transit.

- **Auditing:** Tracking and logging system activity to provide a record of who did what and when. This is crucial for security monitoring and incident response.

- **Conceptual Code Snippet (Python - simulating basic authentication):**

- Python

```python
class AuthManager:

    def __init__(self, credentials):

        self.credentials = credentials


    def authenticate_client(self, client_id, secret):

        if client_id in self.credentials and
self.credentials[client_id] == secret:

            print(f"AuthManager: Client '{client_id}'
authenticated.")

            return True

        else:

            print(f"AuthManager: Authentication failed for client
'{client_id}'.")

            return False
```

```python
    def authorize_action(self, client_id, action, resource):

        # Simulate basic role-based authorization

        if client_id == "ai_model_alpha" and action in
["retrieve", "analyze"] and "customer_data" in resource:

            print(f"AuthManager: Client '{client_id}' authorized to
'{action}' '{resource}'.")

            return True

        else:

            print(f"AuthManager: Client '{client_id}' not
authorized to '{action}' '{resource}'.")

            return False


auth_system = AuthManager({"ai_model_alpha":
"secure_secret_123"})

client_authenticated =
auth_system.authenticate_client("ai_model_alpha",
"secure_secret_123")

if client_authenticated:
```

```
auth_system.authorize_action("ai_model_alpha",
"retrieve", "customer_data")

auth_system.authorize_action("ai_model_alpha",
"delete", "customer_data") # Should fail
```

- ○ **Explanation:** This `AuthManager` simulates basic authentication by checking credentials and authorization based on a client ID, action, and resource. Real-world security systems are far more complex, involving various protocols and policies.

2.3 Introduction to Emerging MCP Server Orientations: Tailoring Intelligence Orchestration

Instead of strict "types," it's more accurate to think about MCP servers as exhibiting different primary orientations based on their core functionalities and the use cases they prioritize. Here are some of these emerging orientations:

1. Data-Centric MCP Servers:

These MCP servers heavily emphasize the management and provision of data to AI models. Their core strength lies in connecting to diverse data sources, potentially transforming and preparing data, and then serving it to AI models in a contextually relevant way via the MCP.

- **Primary Focus:** Data connectivity, data transformation, contextual data delivery to AI.

- **Key Features:** Robust data connectors (for databases, cloud storage, APIs), data indexing and search capabilities, potentially data versioning and lineage tracking, fine-grained access control at the data level.

- **Analogy:** Imagine a highly specialized librarian who not only knows where every book is but can also understand what kind of information an AI researcher needs and prepare relevant excerpts or summaries on demand.

- **Conceptual Code Snippet (Python - illustrating data retrieval with context):**

- Python

```python
class DataCentricMcpServer:

    def __init__(self, data_sources):

        self.data_sources = data_sources


    def process_mcp_request(self, request):

        action = request.get("action")
```

```python
        context = request.get("context")


        if action == "retrieve_data" and context.get("data_source") in
self.data_sources:

            data_source = self.data_sources[context["data_source"]]

            query = context.get("query")

            relevant_context = context.get("context_filters") # Specific
filters provided by AI

            data = data_source.query(query, relevant_context)

            return {"status": "success", "data": data}

        else:

            return {"status": "error", "message": "Invalid request"}


class CustomerDatabase:

    def query(self, sql, filters=None):

        print(f"CustomerDatabase: Executing SQL '{sql}' with filters
'{filters}'")

        # Simulate database interaction based on query and filters
```

```python
        if "product = 'widget'" in sql and filters and filters.get("region")
== "Onitsha":

            return [{"customer_id": 1, "name": "Alice", "region":
"Onitsha"}]

        else:

            return []


db = CustomerDatabase()

data_mcp = DataCentricMcpServer({"customer_database": db})


request = {

    "action": "retrieve_data",

    "context": {

        "data_source": "customer_database",

        "query": "SELECT * FROM customers WHERE product =
'widget'",

        "context_filters": {"region": "Onitsha"}

    }
```

```
}
```

```
response = data_mcp.process_mcp_request(request)
```

```
print(f"Data-Centric MCP Response: {response}")
```

2. Tool-Integration MCP Servers:

These MCP servers focus on providing AI models with access to a variety of external tools and functionalities. They act as a bridge, allowing AI to leverage capabilities beyond their inherent training, such as code execution, API calls to third-party services, or interaction with specialized software.

- **Primary Focus:** Tool connectivity, secure tool execution, abstracting tool complexities for AI.

- **Key Features:** Connectors to various tools (e.g., code interpreters, web browsers, calculators, specialized APIs), sandboxing and security controls for tool execution, potentially workflow orchestration for tool chains.

- **Analogy:** Think of a skilled assistant who knows how to use all sorts of specialized equipment and software, allowing the AI (the principal) to delegate tasks without needing to learn the intricacies of each tool.

- **Conceptual Code Snippet (Python - illustrating tool execution):**

- Python

```python
class ToolIntegrationMcpServer:

    def process_mcp_request(self, request):

        action = request.get("action")

        context = request.get("context")


        if action == "execute_tool" and context.get("tool_name") == "python_executor":

            code = context.get("code")

            result = self._execute_python(code)

            return {"status": "success", "result": result}

        elif action == "execute_tool" and context.get("tool_name") == "web_search":

            query = context.get("query")

            results = self._simulate_web_search(query)

            return {"status": "success", "results": results}
```

```python
        else:

            return {"status": "error", "message": "Invalid tool or
request"}


    def _execute_python(self, code):

        try:

            # Be extremely cautious with eval/exec in production!

            local_vars = {}

            exec(code, globals(), local_vars)

            return local_vars.get("result")

        except Exception as e:

            return f"Error executing Python: {e}"


    def _simulate_web_search(self, query):

        print(f"Simulating web search for '{query}'")

        return ["Result 1 about the query", "Result 2 about the query"]


tool_mcp = ToolIntegrationMcpServer()
```

```python
request_code = {

    "action": "execute_tool",

    "context": {"tool_name": "python_executor", "code": "result = 2 +
2"}

}

response_code = tool_mcp.process_mcp_request(request_code)

print(f"Tool-Integration MCP Response (Code): {response_code}")


request_search = {

    "action": "execute_tool",

    "context": {"tool_name": "web_search", "query": "weather in
Onitsha"}

}

response_search =
tool_mcp.process_mcp_request(request_search)

print(f"Tool-Integration MCP Response (Search):
{response_search}")
```

3. Workflow Orchestration MCP Servers:

These MCP servers focus on enabling AI models to initiate and manage complex workflows involving multiple steps, potentially chaining together data retrieval, tool execution, and interaction with other services. They provide a higher-level abstraction for AI to accomplish more intricate tasks.

- **Primary Focus:** Workflow definition, state management, coordination of multiple services and tools for AI.
- **Key Features:** Workflow definition language or UI, state management for long-running workflows, error handling and retry mechanisms, integration with data and tool connectors.
- **Analogy:** Imagine a project manager who can break down a complex project into a series of tasks, assign those tasks to different teams (services/tools), and track the progress to ensure the overall goal is achieved.
- **Conceptual Illustration:** An AI tasked with writing a report might trigger a workflow: (1) Retrieve relevant data from a database, (2) Analyze the data using a statistical tool, (3) Generate a draft report using a language model, (4) Send the draft for review via email. The Workflow Orchestration MCP server would manage the execution and state of these steps.

4. Hybrid MCP Servers:

It's also likely that many real-world MCP server implementations will be hybrid in nature, combining elements of the above orientations to provide a more comprehensive platform for AI interaction. A single MCP server might manage data access, offer access to various tools, and enable the orchestration of complex AI-driven workflows.

The Evolving Landscape:

It's important to remember that the field of MCP servers is still in its early stages. As the technology matures and adoption grows, we may see more clearly defined categories emerge. The key is to understand the fundamental principles of MCP and how different systems are applying these principles to facilitate intelligent interaction between AI and the digital world.

As you delve into specific MCP server implementations, you'll start to see which of these orientations, or a combination thereof, they emphasize. This understanding will help you leverage their capabilities more effectively.

Chapter 3: Getting Started: Initial Setup and Navigation

Think of this chapter as getting the keys to your new digital office. Before you can start managing things effectively, you need to know how to get in, what tools you have at your disposal, and how to set up your basic workspace.

3.1 Basic Requirements and Prerequisites

Alright, let's get down to the brass tacks of what you'll typically need to have in place before you can start interacting with an MCP server. Think of this as gathering your tools and ensuring your workspace is ready before embarking on a new project. The specific requirements can vary depending on the MCP server implementation you're using (cloud-based vs. self-hosted, specific software dependencies, etc.), but there are some common prerequisites you'll likely encounter.

3.1 Basic Requirements and Prerequisites: Preparing Your MCP Server Environment

Before you can unlock the power of an MCP server, you need to ensure your system meets certain basic criteria. These prerequisites are designed to ensure a smooth and functional experience.

1. Network Connectivity:

- **Requirement:** A stable and reliable internet connection is often essential, especially if you're accessing a cloud-based MCP server or if the server needs to interact with external resources (APIs, data sources). Even for locally hosted servers, network connectivity might be needed for initial setup or communication with other parts of your infrastructure.

- **Analysis:** The bandwidth requirements can vary depending on the volume of data being exchanged and the complexity of the AI interactions. For simple experimentation, a standard broadband connection should suffice. However, for production environments handling large datasets or frequent AI calls, a higher bandwidth connection is recommended.

- **Practical Consideration:** Ensure that your firewall settings (both software and hardware) allow outbound connections to the MCP server's address and port, as well as inbound connections if you're hosting the server yourself and need to access it remotely.

2. Web Browser:

- **Requirement:** Most MCP server implementations provide a web-based user interface for administration, configuration, and monitoring. Therefore, having a modern and up-to-date web browser (e.g., Google Chrome, Mozilla Firefox, Safari, Microsoft Edge) is usually a fundamental requirement.

- **Analysis:** Ensure your browser supports standard web technologies like JavaScript, CSS, and potentially WebSockets for real-time communication with the server. Keeping your browser updated is also crucial for security and compatibility.
- **Practical Consideration:** Some advanced features of the MCP server UI might have specific browser recommendations. Consult the official documentation for any such guidelines.

3. Account Credentials:

- **Requirement:** You will need valid account credentials (usually a username and password) to access the MCP server. For cloud-based services, this involves signing up and creating an account. For self-hosted servers, you'll typically set up an administrator account during the installation process.
- **Analysis:** Securely managing these credentials is paramount. Use strong, unique passwords and consider enabling two-factor authentication if the MCP server offers it.
- **Practical Consideration:** Keep your login details confidential and avoid sharing them. If you're part of a team, ensure proper user management practices are in place.

4. System Resources (for Self-Hosted MCP Servers):

- **Requirement:** If you plan to host the MCP server on your own infrastructure (e.g., a local machine, a virtual machine, or a dedicated server), you'll need to ensure your system meets the minimum hardware and software requirements specified by the MCP server vendor. These typically include:
  - **Operating System:** A supported operating system (e.g., Linux distributions like Ubuntu or CentOS, Windows Server).
  - **CPU:** Minimum processor specifications.
  - **RAM:** Minimum amount of memory required.
  - **Disk Space:** Sufficient storage for the server software, configuration files, logs, and potentially data.
  - **Software Dependencies:** Specific software packages or libraries (e.g., Java Runtime Environment, Python interpreters, database systems) that the MCP server relies on.
- **Analysis:** The actual resource requirements will depend heavily on the expected workload, the number of connected AI models, the volume of data being processed, and the complexity of the services being offered. It's wise to start with the recommended specifications and scale up as needed.
- **Practical Consideration:** Carefully review the official documentation for the specific MCP server you intend to

use to get accurate and up-to-date system requirements. Insufficient resources can lead to performance issues and instability.

5. API Keys or Access Tokens (for External Service Integration):

- **Requirement:** If your intended use of the MCP server involves interacting with external services (e.g., cloud AI platforms, third-party APIs for data or tools), you will likely need API keys or access tokens provided by those services. The MCP server will use these credentials to authenticate and authorize its interactions with these external resources.
- **Analysis:** Treat these API keys and tokens as sensitive information, similar to passwords. Store them securely within the MCP server's configuration and avoid exposing them in client-side code or logs.
- **Practical Consideration:** Understand the usage limits and billing implications associated with the external services you intend to integrate with. Properly manage and rotate API keys as recommended by the service providers.

6. Specific Software or Libraries (for Development):

- **Requirement:** If you plan to develop custom MCP clients (e.g., AI agents that interact with the server) or extend the functionality of the MCP server itself (if the architecture allows for it), you might need specific software development kits (SDKs), libraries, or programming language runtimes (e.g., Python, Java, Node.js).

- **Analysis:** The choice of development tools will depend on the MCP server's API and the programming languages it supports. Familiarity with the relevant SDKs and best practices for interacting with the MCP server's API is crucial.
- **Practical Consideration:** Consult the developer documentation for the MCP server to identify the recommended SDKs and libraries, along with setup instructions and usage examples.

Conceptual Checklist for Beginners:

Before you dive into setting up or using an MCP server, take a moment to check if you have the following in place:

- [ ] A stable internet connection.
- [ ] An up-to-date web browser.
- [ ] Valid account credentials for the MCP server.
- [ ] (If self-hosting) A system that meets the minimum hardware and software requirements.
- [ ] (If integrating with external services) Necessary API keys or access tokens.
- [ ] (If developing) The required SDKs or programming language runtimes.

3.2 Step-by-Step Installation Guide (If Applicable)

Alright, let's walk through the process of installing an MCP server. Now, it's crucial to understand that the *exact* installation steps will vary significantly depending on the specific MCP server software you've chosen. Some might be cloud-based with no local installation needed, while others might offer various installation methods (e.g., package managers, Docker, manual downloads).

Therefore, this guide will provide a **general framework and common considerations** you'll likely encounter. I'll use conceptual examples in a step-by-step manner, highlighting key decisions and potential pitfalls. This section assumes you've determined that your chosen MCP server requires a local installation on your infrastructure.

Step 1: Review the Official Documentation (The Golden Rule)

- **Action:** Locate and thoroughly read the official installation guide for your specific MCP server.
- **Analysis:** This documentation will provide the most accurate system requirements, supported operating systems, and detailed steps tailored to your chosen software. Pay close attention to any prerequisites mentioned (as discussed in section 3.1).

- **Personal Insight:** Skipping this step is like trying to assemble furniture without the instructions – you might get lucky, but you're more likely to end up with a wobbly mess.

Step 2: Choose Your Installation Method

- **Action:** The documentation will likely outline several installation methods. Common options include:
  - **Package Managers (e.g., apt, yum):** For Linux-based systems, the vendor might provide repositories that allow for easy installation using standard package management tools.
  - **Docker:** Many modern applications, including MCP servers, are distributed as Docker containers, simplifying deployment and ensuring consistency across different environments.
  - **Manual Download and Configuration:** This involves downloading an archive (e.g., ZIP, TAR.GZ) and manually configuring the server. This method often requires more technical expertise.
  - **Installation Scripts:** Some vendors provide automated scripts (e.g., shell scripts) to handle the installation process.
- **Analysis:** Consider your technical comfort level and the recommended method for your operating system. Docker often provides the most straightforward and consistent experience. Package managers are convenient for Linux

users. Manual installation offers the most control but requires more manual configuration.

- **Conceptual Illustration:**
  - **Package Manager (Conceptual - Debian/Ubuntu):**
  - Bash

```
sudo apt update

sudo apt install <your-mcp-server-package-name>
```

  -
  - **Docker (Conceptual - assuming a Docker image is available):**
  - Bash

```
docker pull <your-mcp-server/image:latest>

docker run -d --name mcp-server -p <host_port>:<container_port> <your-mcp-server/image:latest>
```

  -
  - **Manual Download (Conceptual - after downloading and extracting):**
  - Bash

```
cd <extracted-directory>

# Follow the instructions in the README or INSTALL file

# This might involve running configuration commands or scripts
```

```
./configure

make

sudo make install
```

Step 3: Download the Necessary Files

- **Action:** If you've chosen a method involving downloading files (manual, script-based, or sometimes even Docker images), proceed to download them from the official source.
- **Analysis:** Always verify the integrity of downloaded files (e.g., using checksums provided by the vendor) to ensure they haven't been tampered with during transit.
- **Practical Consideration:** Be wary of downloading installation files from unofficial sources, as they may contain malware.

Step 4: Execute the Installation Process

- **Action:** Follow the specific instructions for your chosen installation method. This might involve running commands in your terminal, executing an installer application, or running a script.
- **Analysis:** Pay close attention to any prompts or messages during the installation. You might be asked to provide configuration details, such as installation directories, network ports, or initial administrator credentials.
- **Personal Insight:** During my early server setups, I often rushed through the prompts. It's much better to read each

one carefully and understand its implications. Incorrect initial configuration can lead to headaches later.

Step 5: Initial Configuration

- **Action:** After the main installation is complete, you'll likely need to perform some initial configuration. This might involve editing configuration files (e.g., YAML, INI), using a command-line interface, or accessing a web-based setup wizard.

- **Analysis:** This is where you'll set up essential parameters like network settings, database connections (if the MCP server uses one), initial user accounts, and basic security settings.

- **Conceptual Illustration (Conceptual Configuration File - `config.yaml`):**

- YAML

server:

  host: 0.0.0.0

  port: 8080

database:

  type: postgresql

host: localhost

user: mcp_user

password: secure_password

database_name: mcp_db

security:

initial_admin_username: admin

initial_admin_password: strong_initial_password

- You would then need to ensure your PostgreSQL database is running and accessible with the specified credentials.

Step 6: Start the MCP Server

- **Action:** Once the initial configuration is done, you'll need to start the MCP server application or container. The method for starting it will depend on your installation method (e.g., systemctl for Linux services, `docker start` for Docker containers, running an executable).
- **Analysis:** Check the logs or status messages to ensure the server starts without any errors.
- **Conceptual Illustration:**
  - **Systemd (Conceptual - Linux):**
  - Bash

sudo systemctl start <your-mcp-server-service-name>

sudo systemctl status <your-mcp-server-service-name> # Check for errors.

- ○ **Docker (Conceptual):**
- ○ Bash

docker start mcp-server

docker logs mcp-server # View the server logs

Step 7: Verification

- **Action:** After starting the server, you'll need to verify that it's running correctly and accessible. This might involve:
  - ○ Trying to access the web-based interface in your browser using the configured address and port (e.g., `http://your_server_ip:8080`).
  - ○ Using a command-line client or SDK (if provided) to send a basic request to the server.
  - ○ Checking the server logs for any startup errors or unusual activity.
- **Analysis:** Successful verification confirms that the installation and initial configuration were successful.

Step 8: Post-Installation Setup

- **Action:** Once the server is running, you might need to perform additional post-installation steps, such as setting up user accounts, configuring data source connections, or enabling specific services (as discussed in later chapters).

- **Analysis:** Refer to the post-installation section of the official documentation for these steps.

Important Considerations:

- **Permissions:** Ensure the user account running the MCP server has the necessary permissions to access files, directories, and network resources.
- **Firewall Configuration:** Configure your firewall to allow traffic on the ports the MCP server is listening on.
- **Security Best Practices:** Even during installation, start thinking about security. Use strong passwords for initial accounts and consider the network exposure of your server.

Remember, this is a general guide. The specific steps for your chosen MCP server will be detailed in its official documentation. Treat that documentation as your primary source of truth throughout the installation process. Good luck

3.3 Navigating the User Interface (Key Elements and Functions)

Alright, you've successfully installed and started your MCP server (or perhaps you're using a cloud-based version). Now comes the crucial step of understanding how to navigate its user interface. Think of this as familiarizing yourself with the cockpit of a complex machine – knowing where the controls are and what they do is essential for effective operation.

It's important to note that the *specific layout and features* of the user interface will vary significantly depending on the MCP server software you are using. However, there are common elements and functions you'll likely encounter across different implementations. This guide will provide a general overview of these key elements and their typical purposes. For detailed information specific to your MCP server, **always consult the official user manual or documentation.**

3.3 Navigating the User Interface (Key Elements and Functions): Your Command Center

The user interface (UI) is your primary way to interact with the MCP server. It allows you to manage configurations, monitor activity, access logs, and ultimately orchestrate the intelligent interactions with AI models and other resources.

1. Dashboard/Overview:

- **Description:** This is often the first screen you see after logging in. It typically provides a high-level summary of the server's status, key metrics, and recent activity.
- **Typical Elements:** System status indicators (e.g., online/offline), resource usage graphs (CPU, memory,

network), a summary of connected nodes or services, recent logs or alerts, quick access to frequently used sections.

- **Purpose:** To give you an at-a-glance understanding of the server's health and activity.
- **Analogy:** The dashboard of a car, showing your speed, fuel level, engine temperature, and any warning lights.

2. Main Navigation Menu:

- **Description:** Usually located on the side or top of the screen, this menu provides access to the different sections and functionalities of the MCP server.
- **Typical Items:**
  - **Overview/Dashboard:** Returns you to the main summary screen.
  - **Nodes/Agents:** Management of the individual components (physical or virtual) that the MCP server controls or interacts with.
  - **Services/Capabilities:** Configuration and monitoring of the functionalities offered by the MCP server or its managed nodes.
  - **Data Sources/Connectors:** Management of connections to external data repositories.
  - **Tools/Integrations:** Configuration and management of integrations with external tools and services.
  - **Workflows/Automation:** Definition and monitoring of automated tasks and processes.

○ **Security/Access Control:** Management of users, roles, permissions, and security settings.

○ **Configuration/Settings:** Server-wide configuration options.

○ **Logs/Monitoring:** Access to system logs and performance monitoring tools.

○ **API Explorer/Documentation:** Information and tools for interacting with the MCP server's API (for programmatic access).

- **Purpose:** To provide a structured way to access all the features of the MCP server.

- **Analogy:** The main menu of a software application, allowing you to navigate to different features.

3. Lists and Tables:

- **Description:** Many sections of the UI will display information in lists or tables.

- **Typical Features:** Sorting (by clicking on column headers), filtering (to narrow down the displayed items), pagination (for long lists), search functionality (to find specific items), and actions that can be performed on individual items (e.g., edit, delete, view details).

- **Purpose:** To present structured data in an organized and manageable way.

- **Analogy:** A spreadsheet or a database table.

4. Forms and Dialogs:

- **Description:** When you need to configure settings, create new items, or perform actions, you'll often interact with forms and dialog boxes.
- **Typical Elements:** Input fields (for text, numbers, etc.), dropdown menus (for selecting options), checkboxes and radio buttons (for boolean choices), buttons (to submit or cancel), and labels explaining each field.
- **Purpose:** To provide a structured way to input and modify data and settings.
- **Analogy:** Filling out a form online.

5. Buttons and Icons:

- **Description:** These are the primary controls you'll use to initiate actions. Icons often provide a visual representation of the action.
- **Typical Actions:** Add new, edit, delete, save, apply, start, stop, refresh. Hovering over an icon often displays a tooltip explaining its function.
- **Purpose:** To allow you to interact with the UI and trigger actions.
- **Analogy:** The buttons and icons on a toolbar in a desktop application.

6. Search and Filtering:

- **Description:** Essential for quickly finding specific information within the often large datasets managed by an MCP server. Search bars allow you to enter keywords, while filters let you narrow down results based on specific criteria.
- **Purpose:** To improve efficiency and make it easier to locate the information you need.
- **Analogy:** The search bar in a file explorer or the filter options in an email inbox.

7. Contextual Menus:

- **Description:** Sometimes, right-clicking on an item in the UI will bring up a contextual menu with actions relevant to that specific item.
- **Purpose:** To provide quick access to actions related to a specific element.
- **Analogy:** Right-clicking on a file in your operating system's file explorer.

8. Real-time Monitoring Displays:

- **Description:** Some MCP servers offer real-time graphs or charts to visualize metrics like resource usage, network traffic, or the activity of AI models.
- **Purpose:** To provide immediate insights into the server's performance and behavior.

- **Analogy:** Performance monitoring graphs in a system administration tool.

General Tips for Navigation:

- **Explore:** Don't be afraid to click on different menu items and explore the various sections of the UI.
- **Read Labels and Tooltips:** Pay attention to the labels on buttons and fields, and hover over icons to see their descriptions.
- **Look for Documentation Links:** Many UIs provide direct links to the relevant documentation for the section you are currently viewing.
- **Use the Search Function:** If you know what you're looking for, the search function can be a quick way to get there.
- **Follow Tutorials:** The official documentation often includes tutorials that walk you through common tasks using the UI.

Conceptual Example: Navigating to Data Source Configuration

Let's imagine a simplified MCP server UI:

1. **Login:** You open your web browser and navigate to the MCP server's address (e.g., `http://mcp-server.local:8080`) and enter your username and password on the login page.

2. **Dashboard:** After successful login, you land on the Dashboard, which shows the server status as "Online" and displays a graph of CPU usage.

3. **Main Menu:** On the left-hand side, you see a vertical navigation menu. You locate and click on "Data Sources."

4. **Data Sources List:** The main content area now displays a list of currently configured data sources, showing their names and status. There's a button at the top that says "+ Add New Data Source" and a search bar to filter the list.

5. **Adding a New Data Source:** You click on "+ Add New Data Source." A form appears with fields like "Data Source Name," "Type" (dropdown: Database, API, File System), and connection-specific parameters.

6. **Filling the Form:** You enter the required details for the new data source and click the "Save" button at the bottom of the form.

7. **Data Sources List Updated:** You are redirected back to the Data Sources list, and your newly added data source is now visible.

3.4 Basic Configuration for New Users

Alright, you've successfully logged in and navigated the basic layout of your MCP server's user interface. Now, it's time to tailor it to your needs and set up some essential configurations. Think of this as arranging your new office space and setting up your initial preferences to make it functional for your work.

The specific configuration options available will heavily depend on the MCP server you are using. However, there are several common basic configurations that new users often need to address. This guide will walk you through these typical settings with conceptual examples.These initial configurations are crucial for establishing your identity within the system, connecting to the resources you need, and ensuring a secure and functional environment.

1. User Profile and Preferences:

- **Action:** Locate the "Profile," "Account Settings," or similar section in the user interface (often accessible from a dropdown menu associated with your username or an icon in the top right corner).
- **Typical Settings:**
  - **Change Password:** It's highly recommended to change the default password (if any) to a strong, unique one immediately after your first login.
  - **Email Address:** Verify or update your email address, which might be used for notifications, password recovery, and other communications.
  - **Time Zone and Language:** Set your preferred time zone and language for the user interface.
  - **Notification Preferences:** Configure how you want to receive notifications about server events, task completion, or errors.

- **Analysis:** Personalizing your profile ensures you receive relevant information and can securely access the system. A strong password is your first line of defense against unauthorized access.
- **Conceptual Illustration (Conceptual UI Path):** User Menu (Top Right) -> Profile -> Edit Profile

2. Connecting Data Sources:

- **Action:** Navigate to the "Data Sources," "Connections," or "Integrations" section in the main menu.

- **Typical Steps:**

  1. Click on "Add New Data Source" or a similar button.
  2. Choose the type of data source you want to connect to (e.g., Database, API, File System, Cloud Storage).
  3. Fill in the required connection details. This will vary depending on the data source type but might include:
     - **Database:** Server address, port, database name, username, password.
     - **API:** Base URL, API keys, authentication tokens.
     - **File System:** Path to the directory, access credentials (if needed).
     - **Cloud Storage:** Account ID, access keys, bucket name.

4. Click on "Test Connection" (if available) to verify the details are correct.

5. Click "Save" or "Add" to finalize the connection.

- **Analysis:** Connecting to your data sources is essential for enabling AI models and automated tasks to access the information they need. Ensure you have the correct credentials and understand the access permissions required.

- **Conceptual Illustration (Conceptual Python-like interaction with an MCP client):**

- Python

```python
# Assuming 'mcp_client' is an initialized MCP client object

try:

    response = mcp_client.add_data_source(

        name="my_customer_db",

        type="postgresql",

        config={

            "host": "localhost",

            "port": 5432,

            "user": "mcp_user",
```

```
        "password": "secure_db_password",

        "database": "customer_data"

    }

)

if response and response.get("status") == "success":

    print("Data source 'my_customer_db' connected
successfully.")

else:

    print(f"Error connecting data source:
{response.get('message')}")

except Exception as e:

    print(f"An error occurred: {e}")
```

3. Configuring Tool Integrations (If Applicable):

- **Action:** Navigate to the "Tools," "Integrations," or "Services" section.
- **Typical Steps:**
    1. Look for options to "Add New Tool" or "Connect Integration."
    2. Choose the type of tool or service you want to integrate with (e.g., Code Interpreter, Web Search API, Translation Service).

3. Provide any necessary authentication details, such as API keys or access tokens provided by the tool vendor.
4. Configure any tool-specific settings.
5. Save the configuration.

- **Analysis:** Integrating with external tools extends the capabilities of the AI models and automated workflows managed by the MCP server. Securely manage the API keys and understand the usage limits of these tools.

- **Conceptual Illustration (Conceptual UI Path):** Main Menu -> Tools -> Add New Tool -> Select "Web Search API" -> Enter API Key -> Save

4. Setting Up Basic Security Measures:

- **Action:** Navigate to the "Security," "Access Control," or "Users" section.
- **Typical Steps:**
  - **User Management:** Create new user accounts for team members or different AI agents, assigning them appropriate roles and permissions.
  - **Role-Based Access Control (RBAC):** Define roles with specific sets of permissions (e.g., "Data Reader," "Workflow Editor," "Administrator") and assign these roles to users or AI agents.

- ○ **API Key Management:** If AI models or external applications will interact with the MCP server's API, generate and manage API keys, ensuring they have limited scopes and are securely stored.
- ○ **Enabling Two-Factor Authentication (If Available):** Enhance account security by requiring a second verification step during login.
- **Analysis:** Implementing basic security measures is crucial to protect your data and prevent unauthorized access or actions within the MCP server. Follow the principle of least privilege – grant only the necessary permissions.
- **Conceptual Illustration (Conceptual UI Path):** Main Menu -> Security -> Users -> Add New User -> Enter details and assign roles.

5. Configuring Default Settings (Optional):

- **Action:** Explore the "Configuration" or "Settings" section for any default preferences you might want to adjust.
- **Typical Settings:** Default logging levels, notification settings, resource limits, etc.
- **Analysis:** These settings can influence the overall behavior and performance of the MCP server. Understand the implications of each setting before making changes.

Important Considerations for Beginners:

- **Start Simple:** Focus on connecting the essential data sources and configuring basic security first. You can explore more advanced settings later.

- **Refer to Documentation:** Again, the official documentation is your best resource for the specific configuration options and steps for your MCP server.

- **Test Your Connections:** After configuring data sources or tool integrations, always test the connection to ensure it's working correctly.

- **Understand Permissions:** Be mindful of the permissions you grant to users and AI agents. Incorrectly configured permissions can lead to security vulnerabilities or operational issues.

- **Back Up Your Configuration (If Possible):** Once you have a working basic configuration, see if your MCP server provides a way to export or back up its configuration. This can save you time and effort in case of issues.

Chapter 4: Essential Practical Skills for Beginners

Think of this chapter as your first hands-on training session. We'll focus on the fundamental skills you need to start leveraging the power of your MCP server. Remember our office analogy? Now we're going to learn how to use the key tools and services within that office.

4.1 Managing Core Functionality 1: Step-by-Step Guide & Examples

Think of managing data source connections as setting up the pathways for your MCP server to access the various "filing cabinets" where your data resides. This involves adding new connections, editing existing ones, testing their validity, and potentially removing them.

Step 1: Accessing the Data Source Management Section

- **Action (UI):** Navigate to the section labeled "Data Sources," "Connections," "Integrations," or something similar in the main navigation menu of your MCP server's user interface.

- **Analysis:** This section will typically display a list of currently configured data sources and options to add, edit, or delete them.

- **Conceptual Code (MCP Client - Python):**

- Python

```
# Assuming 'mcp_client' is an initialized MCP client object

try:

    response = mcp_client.list_data_sources()

    if response and response.get("status") == "success":

        data_sources = response.get("data")

        if data_sources:

            print("Current Data Sources:")

            for source in data_sources:

                print(f"- Name: {source.get('name')}, Type:
{source.get('type')}, Status: {source.get('status')}")

        else:

            print("No data sources configured yet.")

    else:

        print(f"Error listing data sources: {response.get('message')}")
```

```
except Exception as e:

    print(f"An error occurred: {e}")
```

- **Explanation:** This conceptual code shows how an MCP client might programmatically retrieve a list of configured data sources from the MCP server.

Step 2: Adding a New Data Source

- **Action (UI):** Click on a button labeled "Add New Data Source," "+ Add," "Connect Data Source," or similar.

- **Analysis:** You will be presented with a form asking for details about the data source you want to connect. The specific fields will vary based on the type of data source you choose.

- **Example Fields (Common):**

  - **Name:** A descriptive name for this connection (e.g., "Production Database," "Customer Reviews API").
  - **Type:** A dropdown or selection of the data source type (e.g., PostgreSQL, MySQL, REST API, S3 Bucket).
  - **Connection Parameters:** Specific details required to connect to the chosen type (e.g., host, port, username, password for a database; API endpoint

and keys for an API; bucket name and credentials for cloud storage).

- **Conceptual Code (MCP Client - Python):**

- Python

```python
try:

    response = mcp_client.add_data_source(

        name="marketing_api",

        type="rest_api",

        config={

            "base_url": "https://api.marketing.example.com/v1",

            "api_key": "your_api_key_here",

            "auth_method": "header"

        }

    )

if response and response.get("status") == "success":

    print("Data source 'marketing_api' added successfully.")

else:

    print(f"Error adding data source: {response.get('message')}")
```

```
except Exception as e:

    print(f"An error occurred: {e}")
```

- ○ **Explanation:** This conceptual code demonstrates how an MCP client might programmatically add a new REST API data source, providing a name, type, and configuration details.

Step 3: Configuring Connection Parameters

- **Action (UI):** Carefully fill in all the required connection parameters in the form.
- **Analysis:** Ensure you have the correct credentials and connection details. Typos or incorrect information will lead to connection failures. Refer to the documentation of the specific data source you are trying to connect to for the correct parameters.
- **Personal Insight:** I've often found it helpful to copy and paste sensitive information like passwords or API keys to avoid typing errors, but always ensure you're doing so securely.

Step 4: Testing the Connection

- **Action (UI):** Look for a button labeled "Test Connection," "Verify," or similar and click it.

- **Analysis:** The MCP server will attempt to connect to the data source using the information you provided. A successful test will usually display a confirmation message. If the test fails, you'll receive an error message indicating the likely issue (e.g., incorrect credentials, host not found).

- **Conceptual Code (MCP Client - Python):**

- Python

```
try:
    response =
mcp_client.test_data_source_connection(name="marketing_api")

    if response and response.get("status") == "success":

        print("Connection to 'marketing_api' successful.")

    else:

        print(f"Connection test failed: {response.get('message')}")

except Exception as e:

    print(f"An error occurred: {e}")
```

-
  - **Explanation:** This conceptual code shows how an MCP client might programmatically trigger a connection test for a specific data source.

Step 5: Saving the Data Source Connection

- **Action (UI):** If the connection test is successful (or if there's no explicit test option), click the "Save," "Add," or "Apply" button to finalize the data source configuration.
- **Analysis:** The newly configured data source should now appear in the list of available connections.

Step 6: Editing an Existing Data Source (Optional)

- **Action (UI):** Locate the data source you want to modify in the list and click on an "Edit" button (often represented by a pencil icon).

- **Analysis:** You will be presented with a similar form to the "Add New Data Source" form, pre-filled with the current connection details. You can then modify the parameters as needed and save the changes.

- **Conceptual Code (MCP Client - Python):**

- Python

```python
try:

  response = mcp_client.update_data_source(

    name="marketing_api",

    config={"api_key": "new_api_key_here"}
```

```
)

if response and response.get("status") == "success":

    print("Data source 'marketing_api' updated successfully.")

else:

    print(f"Error updating data source:
{response.get('message')}")

except Exception as e:

    print(f"An error occurred: {e}")
```

- ○ **Explanation:** This conceptual code shows how an MCP client might programmatically update the configuration of an existing data source.

Step 7: Deleting a Data Source (Optional)

- **Action (UI):** Locate the data source you want to remove in the list and click on a "Delete" button (often represented by a trash can icon). You will likely be asked to confirm this action.

- **Analysis:** Deleting a data source connection will prevent the MCP server and its managed AI models from accessing that data source. Proceed with caution.

- **Conceptual Code (MCP Client - Python):**

- Python

```
try:

    response =
mcp_client.delete_data_source(name="marketing_api")

    if response and response.get("status") == "success":

        print("Data source 'marketing_api' deleted successfully.")

    else:

        print(f"Error deleting data source: {response.get('message')}")

except Exception as e:

    print(f"An error occurred: {e}")
```

-

    - **Explanation:** This conceptual code demonstrates how an MCP client might programmatically delete a data source connection.

4.2 Working with Core Functionality 2: Practical Exercises

Alright, building upon our understanding of core functionalities, let's get our hands dirty with some practical exercises. For this "Core Functionality 2," we'll focus on something equally fundamental to many MCP servers: **executing a basic automated task or workflow.** This could involve triggering a predefined action based on a schedule or a specific event.

Again, the exact terminology and steps will vary depending on your MCP server. This guide will provide a general framework and conceptual examples, both in terms of UI interaction and potential programmatic triggers via an MCP client.

Exercise 1: Triggering a Simple Scheduled Task via the UI

Let's imagine your MCP server has a feature to send a daily report via email. Here's how you might interact with it:

Step 1: Accessing the Automation/Workflows Section

- **Action (UI):** Navigate to the section labeled "Automation," "Workflows," "Tasks," "Scheduler," or something similar in the main navigation menu.
- **Analysis:** This section will typically list any existing automated tasks and provide options to create new ones or manage existing ones.

Step 2: Locating the Desired Task

- **Action (UI):** Find the task you want to execute (e.g., "Daily Sales Report Email").
- **Analysis:** The list might show the task's name, description, schedule (if it's scheduled), status (enabled/disabled), and options to manage it.

Step 3: Manually Triggering the Task (If Available)

- **Action (UI):** Look for an option to "Run Now," "Trigger," "Execute," or a similar button associated with the task. Click it.

- **Analysis:** If the MCP server allows manual triggering, this action should initiate the task immediately, regardless of its scheduled execution time. You might see a notification or status update indicating that the task has started or completed.

- **Conceptual Code (MCP Client - Python - triggering a task):**

- Python

```
# Assuming 'mcp_client' is an initialized MCP client object

try:
```

```
response =
mcp_client.trigger_task(task_id="daily_sales_report")

if response and response.get("status") == "success":

    print("Task 'daily_sales_report' triggered successfully.")

    if response.get("details"):

        print(f"Task details: {response.get('details')}")

else:

    print(f"Error triggering task:
{response.get('message')}")

except Exception as e:

    print(f"An error occurred: {e}")
```

- ○ **Explanation:** This conceptual code shows how an MCP client might programmatically trigger a task on the MCP server using a task identifier.

Step 4: Monitoring the Task Execution (UI)

- **Action (UI):** Look for a "Logs," "Activity," or "Task History" section to monitor the progress and outcome of the triggered task.
- **Analysis:** You should be able to see when the task started, any steps it performed, its current status (running,

completed, failed), and potentially any output or logs generated by the task.

Exercise 2: Examining a Scheduled Task's Configuration via the UI

Let's look at how a task that runs automatically is set up:

Step 1: Accessing the Automation/Workflows Section (Same as above)

Step 2: Selecting the Scheduled Task

- **Action (UI):** Find the scheduled task (e.g., "Hourly Data Backup") in the list and click on an "Edit" or "View Details" option.
- **Analysis:** This will open the configuration settings for the task.

Step 3: Understanding the Trigger

- **Action (UI):** Look for a section labeled "Trigger," "Schedule," or "When to Run."

- **Analysis:** This will show how the task is automatically initiated. Common triggers include:

  - ○ **Time-based schedules:** Running at specific times (e.g., daily at 2:00 AM), intervals (e.g., every hour), or using cron expressions.

- ○ **Event-based triggers:** Running when a specific event occurs within the MCP server or an external system.
- **Conceptual Code (MCP Client - Python - retrieving task details):**

- Python

```
try:

  response =
mcp_client.get_task_details(task_id="hourly_data_backup")

  if response and response.get("status") == "success":

    task_details = response.get("details")

    print(f"Details for task 'hourly_data_backup':")

    print(f"- Name: {task_details.get('name')}")

    print(f"- Description: {task_details.get('description')}")

    print(f"- Trigger Type:
{task_details.get('trigger').get('type')}")

    if task_details.get('trigger').get('type') == 'schedule':

      print(f"- Schedule:
{task_details.get('trigger').get('schedule')}")

      print(f"- Actions: {task_details.get('actions')}")
```

```
        print(f"- Status: {task_details.get('status')}")

    else:

        print(f"Error getting task details:
{response.get('message')}")

    except Exception as e:

        print(f"An error occurred: {e}")
```

-

  - **Explanation:** This conceptual code shows how an MCP client might retrieve detailed information about a specific task, including its trigger configuration.

Step 4: Examining the Actions

- **Action (UI):** Look for a section labeled "Actions," "Steps," or "What to Do."
- **Analysis:** This will list the sequence of actions that the task performs when triggered. These actions could include:
  - Retrieving data from a specific data source.
  - Executing a script or code.
  - Calling an external API.
  - Sending an email or notification.
  - Updating a database.
- **Conceptual Illustration:** A task might have actions like: 1. "Fetch data from 'daily_sales' database." 2. "Generate a CSV report." 3. "Email report to [email address removed]."

Step 5: Understanding Parameters and Configuration

- **Action (UI):** For each action, there might be specific parameters or configurations that you can view or edit.
- **Analysis:** This allows you to customize how each step of the automated task behaves (e.g., the specific email address to send to, the API endpoint to call).

Practical Considerations:

- **Permissions:** Ensure the MCP server has the necessary permissions to perform the actions defined in your automated tasks (e.g., access to data sources, ability to send emails).
- **Error Handling:** More advanced automation features might include error handling mechanisms (e.g., retrying failed steps, sending notifications on failure).
- **Logging:** Pay attention to the logs generated by automated tasks to understand their execution flow and identify any issues.

4.3 Understanding and Utilizing Core Functionality 3

Alright, let's delve into our third core functionality. For this example, we'll focus on **interacting with and managing AI models** directly within the MCP server environment. This is a pivotal aspect, as it's where the "intelligent" part of the orchestration truly comes to life.

The capabilities for managing AI models will vary significantly depending on your MCP server. Some might allow you to register pre-trained models, deploy and serve them, monitor their performance, or even fine-tune them. This guide will outline common features you might encounter and provide conceptual Python code snippets to illustrate programmatic interaction via an MCP client.

Step 1: Accessing the AI Model Management Section

- **Action (UI):** Navigate to sections labeled "AI Models," "Models," "Intelligence," or similar in the main menu.
- **Analysis:** This section will typically display a list of available AI models, their status, and options for management.

Step 2: Registering or Adding a New AI Model

- **Action (UI):** Look for buttons like "Add New Model," "Register Model," "Import Model," or similar.

- **Analysis:** You might be presented with different ways to add a model:

    - **Providing a path or URI:** If the model is stored in a specific location (e.g., a cloud storage bucket, a local file system).

- **Selecting from a pre-configured registry:** Some MCP servers might integrate with model registries (like MLflow Model Registry or similar).
- **Connecting to a remote inference endpoint:** If the model is already deployed and serving predictions elsewhere (e.g., on a cloud AI platform).

- **You will likely need to provide metadata about the model, such as:**

  - **Name/ID:** A unique identifier for the model within the MCP server.
  - **Type/Framework:** The type of AI model (e.g., Large Language Model, Computer Vision Model, Tabular Model) and the framework it's built on (e.g., TensorFlow, PyTorch, scikit-learn).
  - **Version:** The version of the model.
  - **Description:** A brief description of the model's purpose.
  - **Input/Output Schema:** Information about the expected input format and the structure of the model's predictions.

- **Conceptual Code (MCP Client - Python - registering a model):**

- Python

```
# Assuming 'mcp_client' is an initialized MCP client object
```

```python
try:

    response = mcp_client.register_model(

        name="sentiment_analyzer_v1",

        model_type="text_classification",

        framework="pytorch",

        location="s3://my-model-bucket/sentiment_v1.pt",

        input_schema={"text": "string"},

        output_schema={"sentiment": "string", "confidence":
"float"},

        description="A model for analyzing sentiment of text."

    )

    if response and response.get("status") == "success":

        model_id = response.get("model_id")

        print(f"Model 'sentiment_analyzer_v1' registered
successfully with ID: {model_id}")

    else:

        print(f"Error registering model:
{response.get('message')}")
```

```
except Exception as e:

    print(f"An error occurred: {e}")
```

- ○ **Explanation:** This conceptual code shows how an MCP client might programmatically register a pre-trained PyTorch model located in an S3 bucket, along with its metadata.

Step 3: Deploying or Serving an AI Model

- **Action (UI):** Once a model is registered, you might need to deploy it to make it available for inference (getting predictions). Look for options like "Deploy," "Serve," "Activate," or similar associated with the model.
- **Analysis:** Deployment might involve:

  - ○ Allocating computational resources (CPU, GPU) to run the model.
  - ○ Creating an API endpoint that can be called to get predictions.
  - ○ Managing the lifecycle of the deployed model (starting, stopping, scaling).

- **Conceptual Code (MCP Client - Python - deploying a model):**

- Python

```
try:
```

```python
        response =
mcp_client.deploy_model(model_id="sentiment_analyzer_v
1", deployment_config={"instance_type": "cpu",
"replica_count": 1})

    if response and response.get("status") == "success":

        deployment_url = response.get("endpoint_url")

        print(f"Model 'sentiment_analyzer_v1' deployed
successfully at: {deployment_url}")

    else:

        print(f"Error deploying model:
{response.get('message')}")

except Exception as e:

    print(f"An error occurred: {e}")
```

-
    - **Explanation:** This conceptual code shows how an
      MCP client might programmatically request the
      deployment of a registered model, specifying
      deployment configurations like instance type and the
      number of replicas.

Step 4: Interacting with Deployed AI Models (Getting Predictions)

- **Action (UI):** Some MCP servers might provide a built-in interface to test or interact with deployed models by providing input data.

- **Conceptual Code (MCP Client - Python - getting a prediction):**

- Python

```python
try:

    response = mcp_client.predict(

        model_id="sentiment_analyzer_v1",

        inputs={"text": "This is a fantastic product!"}

    )

    if response and response.get("status") == "success":

        prediction = response.get("prediction")

        print(f"Prediction: {prediction}")

    else:

        print(f"Error getting prediction:
{response.get('message')}")
```

```
except Exception as e:

    print(f"An error occurred: {e}")
```

- Explanation: This conceptual code shows how an MCP client might send input data to a deployed model and receive a prediction in response.

Step 5: Monitoring AI Model Performance

- **Action (UI):** Look for sections like "Monitoring," "Metrics," or "AI Model Dashboard" to track the performance of your deployed models.

- **Analysis:** You might see metrics such as:

  - **Latency:** The time it takes for the model to return a prediction.
  - **Throughput:** The number of predictions the model can handle per unit of time.
  - **Resource Utilization:** CPU and memory usage of the model's deployment.
  - **Accuracy Metrics:** Depending on the model type, you might see metrics like accuracy, precision, recall, F1-score, etc.

- **Conceptual Code (MCP Client - Python - retrieving model metrics):**

- Python

```python
try:
    response = mcp_client.get_model_metrics(model_id="sentiment_analyzer_v1", metrics=["latency", "throughput", "cpu_utilization"])
    if response and response.get("status") == "success":
        metrics = response.get("metrics")
        print(f"Metrics for 'sentiment_analyzer_v1': {metrics}")
    else:
        print(f"Error getting model metrics: {response.get('message')}")
except Exception as e:
    print(f"An error occurred: {e}")
```

-
    - **Explanation:** This conceptual code shows how an MCP client might retrieve performance metrics for a deployed model.

Step 6: Managing Model Lifecycle (Updating, Undeploying, Deleting)

- **Action (UI):** You should find options to update a deployed model with a new version, undeploy (stop serving) a model, or delete a registered model.

- **Analysis:** These actions allow you to manage the lifecycle of your AI assets within the MCP server.

- **Conceptual Code (MCP Client - Python - undeploying a model):**

- Python

```
try:

    response =
mcp_client.undeploy_model(model_id="sentiment_analyzer
_v1")

    if response and response.get("status") == "success":

        print(f"Model 'sentiment_analyzer_v1' undeployed
successfully.")

    else:

        print(f"Error undeploying model:
{response.get('message')}")
```

```
except Exception as e:

    print(f"An error occurred: {e}")
```

-
    o **Explanation:** This conceptual code shows how an MCP client might programmatically request the undeployment of a model.

4.4 Simple Automation Tasks (If Applicable)

Alright, let's explore the realm of simple automation tasks within your MCP server. This is where you can begin to offload repetitive activities and let the system work for you. The capabilities for automation will vary, but many MCP servers offer ways to define and execute basic sequences of actions based on triggers like schedules or specific events.

This guide will walk you through the typical steps involved in creating and managing simple automation tasks using the MCP server's user interface, along with conceptual Python code snippets to illustrate programmatic interaction via an MCP client.

Step 1: Accessing the Automation/Workflows Section (Revisited)

- **Action (UI):** Navigate to the section labeled "Automation," "Workflows," "Tasks," "Rules," or something similar in the main navigation menu.

- **Analysis:** This section will typically list existing automation tasks and provide options to create new ones.

Step 2: Creating a New Automation Task

- **Action (UI):** Click on buttons like "Add New Automation," "Create Task," "+ New Rule," or similar.
- **Analysis:** You'll likely be guided through a process to define the task, which generally involves:
  - **Naming the Task:** Give your automation a descriptive name (e.g., "Daily Data Backup," "Low Inventory Alert").
  - **Defining a Trigger:** Specify what initiates the task. Common triggers include:
    - **Schedule-based:** Run at a specific time or interval (e.g., every day at 6 AM).
    - **Event-based:** Run when a certain event occurs within the system (e.g., a new data point is received, a threshold is reached).
  - **Defining Actions:** Specify the sequence of actions to be performed when the trigger occurs.

Step 3: Configuring the Trigger

- **Action (UI):** Select the type of trigger you want and configure its details.

- **Example Triggers and Configurations:**

- Schedule: Select a frequency (e.g., Daily, Weekly, Monthly), specify the time (e.g., 06:00), and potentially choose specific days. Some systems might use cron-like expressions for more complex schedules.
  - Event: Choose the type of event to listen for (e.g., "New Customer Order Created," "Sensor Reading Exceeds Threshold"). You might need to specify additional criteria for the event.
- **Conceptual Code (MCP Client - Python - creating a scheduled task):**

- Python

```python
# Assuming 'mcp_client' is an initialized MCP client object

try:

  response = mcp_client.create_task(

    name="daily_backup",

    description="Runs a daily backup of critical data at 3 AM.",

    trigger={

      "type": "schedule",

      "schedule": "0 3 * * *"  # Cron expression for 3:00 AM daily

    },
```

```python
    actions=[

        {"type": "execute_script", "script_path":
"/opt/backup/backup.sh"},

        {"type": "send_notification", "recipient":
"admin@example.com", "message": "Daily backup completed."}

    ],

    enabled=True

  )

  if response and response.get("status") == "success":

    task_id = response.get("task_id")

    print(f"Task 'daily_backup' created successfully with ID:
{task_id}")

  else:

    print(f"Error creating task: {response.get('message')}")

except Exception as e:

  print(f"An error occurred: {e}")
```

- **Explanation:** This conceptual code shows how an MCP client might programmatically create a scheduled task defined by a cron expression, with two actions: executing a script and sending an email notification.

Step 4: Defining the Actions

- **Action (UI):** Add and configure the actions that should occur when the trigger is activated.

- **Common Action Types and Configurations:**

  - **Send Notification:** Specify the recipient(s), subject, and body of the notification (e.g., email, SMS, webhook).
  - **Execute Script:** Provide the path to a script to be executed (e.g., shell script, Python script). You might need to configure parameters or working directories.
  - **Call API Endpoint:** Specify the URL, HTTP method (GET, POST, etc.), headers, and body for an API call.
  - **Update Data:** Define how data should be modified in a connected data source.
  - **Trigger Another Task:** Initiate another predefined automation task.
- **Conceptual Code (MCP Client - Python - creating an event-based task):**

- Python

try:

```python
response = mcp_client.create_task(

    name="low_inventory_alert",

    description="Sends an alert when inventory of a product
drops below a threshold.",

    trigger={

        "type": "event",

        "event_name": "inventory_level_changed",

        "criteria": {"product_id": "widget-123", "new_level": "< 10"}

    },

    actions=[

        {"type": "send_notification", "recipient":
"inventory@example.com", "message": "Low inventory for product
widget-123. Current level: {{event.new_level}}"},

        {"type": "log_event", "message": "Low inventory alert
triggered for widget-123"}

    ],

    enabled=True

)

if response and response.get("status") == "success":
```

```
    task_id = response.get("task_id")

    print(f"Task 'low_inventory_alert' created successfully with ID:
{task_id}")

  else:

    print(f"Error creating task: {response.get('message')}")

except Exception as e:

  print(f"An error occurred: {e}")
```

- ○ **Explanation:** This conceptual code shows how an
  MCP client might create an event-based task that
  triggers when an "inventory_level_changed" event
  occurs for a specific product with a new level below
  10. It defines actions to send a notification and log
  the event. Note the use of `{{event.new_level}}`
  for accessing event data within the notification
  message.

Step 5: Enabling the Automation Task

- **Action (UI):** Look for a toggle switch or a status setting
  (e.g., "Enabled/Disabled") for your newly created task and
  ensure it is set to "Enabled" or "Active."
- **Analysis:** An enabled task will be monitored for its trigger
  condition and will execute its actions when the trigger
  occurs.

Step 6: Monitoring Task Execution (Revisited)

- **Action (UI):** Use the "Logs," "Activity," or "Task History" section to monitor when your automated tasks are triggered and the outcome of their actions.
- **Analysis:** Reviewing logs is crucial for troubleshooting and ensuring your automation is working as expected.

Practical Considerations for Simple Automation:

- **Keep it Focused:** Start with simple, well-defined tasks. Don't try to automate overly complex workflows initially.
- **Test Thoroughly:** After creating an automation, test it to ensure it triggers correctly and performs the intended actions without errors.
- **Error Handling:** Consider what should happen if an action within the automation fails. Some systems offer basic error handling options.
- **Variables and Context:** More advanced automation systems might allow you to use variables or access contextual information (e.g., data from the triggering event) within the actions.

Chapter 5: Integrating with AI via MCP

We've primarily focused on the MCP server as a central management hub. Now, we'll see how it becomes a gateway for AI to access and utilize the resources it orchestrates. This integration is a key aspect of modern MCP servers and opens up a world of possibilities for intelligent automation and data utilization.

5.1 How MCP Enables AI Interaction: A Beginner's Perspective

Alright, let's zoom in on the magic behind the scenes: how exactly does an MCP server facilitate interaction with Artificial Intelligence? For beginners, the idea of AI talking to other systems might seem like something out of a sci-fi movie. But the reality, while sophisticated, is built on logical principles that become clear with a simple analogy.

Think of an AI model as a highly skilled specialist – perhaps a brilliant data analyst or a gifted writer. This specialist possesses incredible abilities within their domain but might struggle to navigate the complexities of the broader organization (our digital world). They don't inherently know how to access specific databases, use particular software tools, or communicate their findings in a standardized way that everyone understands.

This is where the MCP server steps in. It acts as a **knowledgeable intermediary and a standardized communication hub** specifically designed to help AI models interact with the external world effectively.

The MCP as a Translator and Guide:

1. **Standardized Language (The MCP Protocol):** Just like our specialist needs a common language to communicate with different departments, AI models need a standardized way to express their needs and receive information. The Model Context Protocol (MCP) provides this language. It defines the structure and format for AI models to make requests (e.g., "retrieve customer data," "analyze this text," "execute this code") and for the MCP server to respond (e.g., with the requested data, the analysis results, or the output of the executed code).

    o **Conceptual Analogy:** Imagine the MCP protocol as a set of well-defined forms and procedures that every department in our organization understands. The AI specialist fills out these forms to request specific actions or information.

2. **Contextual Understanding:** AI models often need to interact with the world based on specific context. The MCP protocol allows AI to include this context in its requests (e.g., "retrieve orders for *this specific customer*," "analyze the sentiment of *this particular email*"). The MCP server is

designed to understand and leverage this context when fulfilling the AI's requests.

- ○ **Conceptual Analogy:** Our AI specialist can specify the project code or client name on the request form, allowing the relevant department to provide information specific to that context.

3. **Simplified Access to Resources:** Instead of an AI model needing to understand the intricate details of how to connect to a dozen different databases or APIs, the MCP server provides a unified point of access. The AI model simply makes a request through the MCP, and the server handles the underlying complexities of connecting to the appropriate resource.

- ○ **Conceptual Analogy:** The MCP server acts as a central switchboard operator. The AI specialist doesn't need to know the direct phone number for every department; they just call the operator (MCP server) and specify who they need to reach and what they need.

4. **Capability Discovery:** Ideally, an MCP server can even help AI models discover what resources and capabilities are available. An AI might ask, "What tools do you have for analyzing customer feedback?" and the MCP server can respond with a list of available services (e.g., sentiment

analysis model, topic extraction tool).

- ○ **Conceptual Analogy:** Our AI specialist can consult an internal directory (managed by the MCP server) to find out what services and tools are available within the organization.

Conceptual Code Illustration (Python - A Simplified Interaction):

Let's imagine a very basic interaction where an AI model wants to get the current weather in a specific city using an MCP server that has access to a weather API.

Python

```
# Assume a simplified MCP client library


class McpClient:

    def __init__(self, server_address):

        self.server_address = server_address


    def send_request(self, request):

        print(f"Sending MCP request to {self.server_address}: {request}")
```

```python
        # In a real system, this would involve network communication

        return self._simulate_server_response(request)


    def _simulate_server_response(self, request):

        action = request.get("action")

        context = request.get("context")


        if action == "get_weather" and "city" in context:

            city = context["city"]

            if city.lower() == "onitsha":

                return {"status": "success", "weather": {"temperature":
28, "conditions": "Sunny"}}

            else:

                return {"status": "success", "weather": {"temperature":
25, "conditions": "Cloudy"}}

        else:

            return {"status": "error", "message": "Invalid request"}
```

```python
# Our AI model (simplified)

class AiModel:

    def __init__(self, mcp_client):

        self.mcp_client = mcp_client


    def get_current_weather(self, city):

        request = {

            "model_id": "weather_ai_v1",

            "action": "get_weather",

            "context": {"city": city}

        }

        response = self.mcp_client.send_request(request)

        if response and response.get("status") == "success":

            return response.get("weather")

        else:

            return f"Error: {response.get('message')}"
```

```
# Setting up the interaction

mcp_server_address = "http://mcp-server:8080"

mcp_client = McpClient(mcp_server_address)

weather_ai = AiModel(mcp_client)


# The AI model asks for the weather

weather = weather_ai.get_current_weather("Onitsha")

print(f"Current weather in Onitsha: {weather}")



weather = weather_ai.get_current_weather("Lagos")

print(f"Current weather in Lagos: {weather}")
```

In this simplified example:

- The `AiModel` doesn't need to know how to directly call a weather API.
- It formulates its request in a standardized MCP format (`action`: "get_weather", `context`: {"city": ...}).
- The `McpClient` handles sending this request to the `McpServer`.

- The `McpServer` (simulated here) understands the MCP request, accesses the weather information (again, simulated), and returns a standardized response.

This illustrates the fundamental role of the MCP server: to abstract away the complexities of the underlying infrastructure and provide a consistent, context-aware communication layer that enables AI models to interact seamlessly with the digital world. As AI becomes more integrated into various systems, this kind of standardized and intelligent interaction management will become increasingly crucial.

5.2 Basic Examples of AI Leveraging MCP Server Capabilities

Alright, let's solidify our understanding of how AI models can leverage the capabilities of an MCP server with some basic, relatable examples. Think of these scenarios as simple use cases where an AI, through the MCP, can extend its abilities by interacting with the managed resources. While providing fully working, end-to-end code examples that connect to real-world AI models and MCP servers would be complex and require specific platform setups, I can illustrate these interactions with conceptual Python code snippets that highlight the core principles.

In these examples, we'll see how an AI model, equipped with an MCP client, can perform tasks that would be impossible or significantly more difficult without the MCP server acting as an intermediary.

Example 1: AI Retrieving Contextual Data for Question Answering

Imagine an AI chatbot designed to answer questions about products in an online store. The AI itself might have been trained on a large corpus of text, but it doesn't inherently know the real-time inventory levels or detailed specifications of the current product catalog.

- **How MCP Helps:** The MCP server has a connection to the store's product database. The AI, when asked a question about a specific product, can use the MCP to request this information.

- **Conceptual Interaction:**

- Python

```python
class ProductInfoAi:

    def __init__(self, mcp_client):

        self.mcp_client = mcp_client
```

```python
    def answer_product_query(self, product_name,
user_question):

        # 1. AI identifies the need for product-specific data

        if "specifications" in user_question.lower() or
"availability" in user_question.lower():

            # 2. AI formulates an MCP request for product
details

            request = {

                "model_id": self.__class__.__name__,

                "action": "retrieve_product_details",

                "context": {"product_name": product_name}

            }

            response = self.mcp_client.send_request(request)

            if response and response.get("status") ==
"success":

                product_data = response.get("data")

                if product_data:

                    return self._generate_answer(user_question,
product_data)
```

```python
        else:

            return f"Sorry, I couldn't find details for
'{product_name}'."

        else:

        return f"Error retrieving product details:
{response.get('message')}"

    else:

        # If the question is general, the AI might answer
from its internal knowledge

        return
self._generate_general_answer(user_question,
product_name)



    def _generate_answer(self, question, data):

        # Simple logic to formulate an answer based on the
retrieved data

        if "specifications" in question.lower():

            return f"The specifications for {data.get('name')}
include: {data.get('specs')}"

        elif "availability" in question.lower():
```

```python
        return f"The current availability for {data.get('name')}
is: {data.get('availability')}"

        return "I can provide more details if you ask a more
specific question."


    def _generate_general_answer(self, question,
product_name):

        return f"Regarding '{product_name}', what specifically
would you like to know?"



# Assume mcp_client is initialized

product_ai = ProductInfoAi(mcp_client)



# User asks a question that requires external data

response = product_ai.answer_product_query("Awesome
T-Shirt", "What are the available sizes?")

print(response)



response = product_ai.answer_product_query("Awesome
T-Shirt", "Tell me more about it.")
```

```
print(response)
```

- **MCP Server-Side (Conceptual):** The MCP server would receive the request with the action "retrieve_product_details" and the product name in the context. It would then query the product database and return the relevant information (specifications, availability, etc.) in the response.

Example 2: AI Utilizing a Tool via MCP for Calculations

Consider an AI agent that needs to perform mathematical calculations as part of its task, but it doesn't have inherent calculation abilities.

- **How MCP Helps:** The MCP server has access to a "Calculator" tool (perhaps a code interpreter or a dedicated calculation service).[2] The AI can use the MCP to request the execution of this tool with the necessary parameters.[3]

- **Conceptual Interaction:**

- Python

```
class MathAi:

    def __init__(self, mcp_client):
```

```python
        self.mcp_client = mcp_client


    def solve_equation(self, equation):
        # 1. AI identifies the need for calculation
        if any(op in equation for op in ["+", "-", "*", "/"]):
            # 2. AI formulates an MCP request to execute the
calculator tool
            request = {
                "model_id": self.__class__.__name__,
                "action": "execute_tool",
                "context": {"tool_name": "calculator", "expression":
equation}
            }
            response = self.mcp_client.send_request(request)
            if response and response.get("status") ==
"success":
                result = response.get("result")
                return f"The result of '{equation}' is: {result}"
```

```python
        else:

            return f"Error executing calculator:
{response.get('message')}"

    else:

        return "That doesn't look like an equation I can
solve."


# Assume mcp_client is initialized

math_ai = MathAi(mcp_client)


# AI needs to solve an equation

result = math_ai.solve_equation("15 * 3 + (20 / 4)")

print(result)


result = math_ai.solve_equation("What is the capital of
Nigeria?")

print(result)
```

- ○ **MCP Server-Side (Conceptual):** The MCP server would receive the request to "execute_tool" with the tool name "calculator" and the mathematical expression in the context. It would then invoke the calculator service, pass the expression, get the result, and return it in the response.

Example 3: AI Triggering an Automation Workflow via MCP

Imagine an AI that, upon detecting a critical event (e.g., a high-priority customer complaint), needs to initiate a predefined workflow to address it.

- **How MCP Helps:** The MCP server manages various automated workflows.[4] The AI can use the MCP to trigger a specific workflow by its identifier.

- **Conceptual Interaction:**

- Python

```python
class ComplaintAi:

    def __init__(self, mcp_client):

        self.mcp_client = mcp_client


    def handle_complaint(self, complaint_text, customer_id):
```

```python
        if "urgent" in complaint_text.lower() or "critical" in
complaint_text.lower():

            # 1. AI identifies a critical complaint

            print("Critical complaint detected. Initiating
escalation workflow.")

            # 2. AI formulates an MCP request to trigger the
escalation workflow

            request = {

                "model_id": self.__class__.__name__,

                "action": "trigger_workflow",

                "context": {"workflow_id":
"escalate_critical_complaint", "customer_id": customer_id,
"complaint_details": complaint_text}

            }

            response = self.mcp_client.send_request(request)

            if response and response.get("status") ==
"success":

                return "Complaint escalation initiated."

            else:
```

```python
        return f"Error triggering workflow: {response.get('message')}"

    else:

        return "Acknowledging complaint. It will be addressed shortly."


# Assume mcp_client is initialized

complaint_ai = ComplaintAi(mcp_client)


# AI processes a complaint

response = complaint_ai.handle_complaint("This is URGENT! My order is missing!", "user123")

print(response)


response = complaint_ai.handle_complaint("I have a question about my order.", "user456")

print(response)
```

- **MCP Server-Side (Conceptual):** The MCP server would receive the request to "trigger_workflow" with the workflow ID and relevant context (customer ID, complaint details). It would then initiate the "escalate_critical_complaint" workflow, which might involve notifying support staff, creating a ticket, etc.

These basic examples illustrate the power of an MCP server in enabling AI models to interact with and leverage the broader digital ecosystem. By providing a standardized communication layer and managing access to various resources and capabilities, the MCP server significantly enhances the potential and practicality of AI applications. As AI continues to evolve, this kind of intelligent orchestration will become increasingly vital.

5.3 Understanding Data Flow Between AI and MCP Server

Alright, let's trace the pathways of information as AI models interact with an MCP server. Understanding this data flow is crucial for grasping how AI can effectively utilize the resources managed by the MCP. Think of it as understanding the delivery routes between our AI specialist and the central information hub.

The interaction between an AI model and an MCP server typically follows a request-response pattern, much like a client-server architecture. Data flows in both directions, each carrying specific types of information.

1. AI Model to MCP Server (The Request):

When an AI model needs to access a resource or perform an action managed by the MCP server, it sends a request. This request, formatted according to the Model Context Protocol (MCP), generally includes the following components:

- **Model Identification (`model_id`):** Identifies the AI model making the request. This can be useful for authentication, authorization, and logging.
- **Action (`action`):** Specifies what the AI wants the MCP server to do. Examples include `retrieve_data`, `execute_tool`, `trigger_workflow`, `get_model_prediction`.
- **Context (`context`):** Provides specific details and parameters relevant to the requested action. This is where the AI provides the necessary information for the server to understand and fulfill the request. The structure of the context will vary depending on the action. For example:
  - For `retrieve_data`: Context might include the `data_source` name and a `query`.
  - For `execute_tool`: Context might include the `tool_name` and input `parameters`.
  - For `get_model_prediction`: Context would contain the input data for the AI model.

- **Response Format (`response_format` - Optional):** The AI might specify the desired format for the response (e.g., `json`, `csv`, `text`).
- **Authentication/Authorization Details (Implicit or Explicit):** The request might implicitly or explicitly include credentials (e.g., API keys, tokens) to authenticate the AI model and authorize the requested action.

Conceptual Code Illustration (Python - AI Sending a Request):

Python

```python
class ImageRecognitionAi:

    def __init__(self, mcp_client):

        self.mcp_client = mcp_client


    def analyze_image(self, image_url):
        request = {

            "model_id": self.__class__.__name__,

            "action": "analyze_image",

            "context": {"image_url": image_url},

            "response_format": "json"
```

```
    }

    response = self.mcp_client.send_request(request)

    return response


# Assume mcp_client is initialized

image_ai = ImageRecognitionAi(mcp_client)

analysis_result =
image_ai.analyze_image("http://example.com/cat.jpg")

print(analysis_result)
```

In this example, the `ImageRecognitionAi` sends a request to the MCP server with the action `analyze_image` and the URL of the image to be analyzed in the context. It also specifies that it expects the response in JSON format.

2. MCP Server to AI Model (The Response):

Once the MCP server processes the AI's request, it sends back a response. This response typically includes:

- **Status (`status`):** Indicates whether the request was successful (`success`) or if an error occurred (`error`).
- **Data (`data` - On Success):** Contains the information requested by the AI. The format of this data will depend on

the action and the `response_format` specified in the request (or a default format). For example:

- For `retrieve_data`: `data` might be a list of dictionaries or a CSV string.
- For `execute_tool`: `data` might contain the output of the tool execution.
- For `get_model_prediction`: `data` would contain the prediction from the AI model managed by the MCP server.

- **Result (`result` - On Success):** Similar to `data`, but might be used for simpler responses or the direct output of an action.

- **Message (`message` - On Error):** Provides a description of the error that occurred.

- **Details (`details` - Optional):** May include additional information about the request processing or the response.

Conceptual Code Illustration (Python - MCP Server Simulating a Response):

Python

```
# (Continuing from the previous example)


class MockMcpServer:

    def process_request(self, request):
```

```python
        action = request.get("action")

        context = request.get("context")


        if action == "analyze_image" and "image_url" in context:

            image_url = context["image_url"]

            if "cat.jpg" in image_url:

                return {"status": "success", "data": {"labels": ["cat",
"animal"], "confidence": [0.95, 0.98]}}

            else:

                return {"status": "success", "data": {"labels": ["dog",
"animal"], "confidence": [0.92, 0.97]}}

        else:

            return {"status": "error", "message": "Invalid request or
action"}


# Simulate the MCP server processing the AI's request

mock_server = MockMcpServer()
```

```python
server_response =
mock_server.process_request(image_ai.analyze_image("http://exa
mple.com/cat.jpg"))

print(f"MCP Server Response: {server_response}")


server_response =
mock_server.process_request(image_ai.analyze_image("http://exa
mple.com/dog.jpg"))

print(f"MCP Server Response: {server_response}")
```

In this simplified simulation, the `MockMcpServer` receives the request, processes the `analyze_image` action based on the `image_url` in the context, and returns a JSON response containing the analysis results (labels and confidence scores).

Key Aspects of Data Flow:

- **Structured Communication:** The MCP protocol ensures that the data exchanged between the AI and the server is structured and predictable, facilitating easy parsing and utilization on both sides.
- **Contextual Relevance:** The `context` in the request allows the AI to provide specific information, ensuring that

the server provides data or performs actions relevant to the AI's current needs.

- **Abstraction:** The AI doesn't need to know the underlying mechanisms of how the server retrieves data or executes tools. It simply makes a request according to the MCP, and the server handles the complexities.
- **Security Considerations:** The data flow must be secure, especially when sensitive information is being exchanged. MCP implementations often include mechanisms for authentication, authorization, and encryption.
- **Efficiency:** The design of the MCP protocol and the server's architecture aims for efficient data transfer and processing to minimize latency in AI interactions.

Chapter 6: Basic Troubleshooting and Maintenance

No matter how user-friendly a system is, you're bound to encounter a few bumps along the road. This chapter will help you identify and resolve some common issues that beginners might face with their MCP server. We'll also cover simple ways to monitor its health and essential maintenance routines to prevent problems in the first place.

6.1 Identifying and Resolving Common Beginner Issues

Alright, as you start your journey with MCP servers and AI integration, it's natural to encounter a few bumps along the road. Think of these as learning opportunities – each challenge you overcome will deepen your understanding. This section will highlight some common issues that beginners often face and provide guidance on how to identify and resolve them. While providing complete, working code examples for every potential issue is impossible due to the variety of MCP server implementations, I'll offer conceptual examples and troubleshooting strategies.

Let's equip you with some common problem-solving techniques for navigating the initial learning curve.

1. Connection Errors (AI Client to MCP Server):

- **Symptom:** Your AI client (the code or application trying to communicate with the MCP server) fails to connect, resulting in errors like "Connection refused," "Timeout," or "Host not found."
- **Possible Causes:**
    1. **Incorrect Server Address or Port:** Double-check the server address (IP address or hostname) and the port number you've configured in your client application.
    2. **Firewall Issues:** Your local firewall or a network firewall might be blocking communication on the specified port.
    3. **Server Not Running:** Ensure that the MCP server process is actually running on the server machine.
    4. **Network Connectivity Problems:** Check your internet connection or network configuration.
- **Troubleshooting Steps:**
    1. **Verify Server Address and Port:** Carefully compare the configured address and port in your client with the server's settings (often found in its configuration files or UI).
    2. **Test Network Connectivity:** Use tools like `ping` (to check if you can reach the server's IP address) and `telnet` or `nc` (to check if you can connect to the server's port) from your client machine.

- **Conceptual Example (Terminal):**
- Bash

```
ping <mcp_server_ip_or_hostname>

telnet <mcp_server_ip_or_hostname>
<mcp_server_port>

# or

nc -zv <mcp_server_ip_or_hostname>
<mcp_server_port>
```

3. **Check Server Status:** If you have access to the server machine, verify that the MCP server process is running (e.g., using `ps aux | grep <mcp_server_process_name>` on Linux or Task Manager on Windows).

4. **Review Firewall Rules:** Check the firewall settings on both your client machine and the server to ensure that traffic on the MCP server's port is allowed in both directions.

- **Personal Insight:** I've spent hours debugging connection issues only to find a simple typo in the server address. Always double-check the basics.

2. Authentication/Authorization Failures:

- **Symptom:** Your AI client connects to the server but receives errors like "Unauthorized," "Forbidden," or "Invalid credentials."

- **Possible Causes:**

  1. **Incorrect Credentials:** Double-check the API keys, tokens, usernames, and passwords you are using to authenticate.
  2. **Expired Credentials:** Some authentication tokens have a limited lifespan. You might need to refresh them.
  3. **Insufficient Permissions:** The authenticated user or AI model might not have the necessary permissions to perform the requested action or access the requested resource.

- **Troubleshooting Steps:**

  1. **Verify Credentials:** Ensure you are using the correct and up-to-date authentication credentials.
  2. **Review Server Logs:** Check the MCP server's logs for details about the authentication failure. They might provide more specific error messages or indicate which credentials were rejected.
  3. **Check User/Role Permissions (via UI or Admin Tools):** If you have administrative access to the MCP server, verify the permissions associated with the user account or API key your AI client is using.

4. **Credential Refresh Mechanism:** If your authentication method involves tokens, ensure your client is correctly handling token expiration and renewal.

- **Conceptual Example (Python - potential error handling in the client):**

- Python

```
try:

    response =
mcp_client.send_request(request_with_credentials)

    if response.get("status") == "error" and
response.get("message") == "Unauthorized":

        print("Authentication failed. Please check your
credentials.")

        # Potentially attempt to refresh token if
applicable

    elif response.get("status") == "error" and
response.get("message") == "Forbidden":

        print("You do not have permission to perform
this action.")

    else:
```

```
# Process the successful response

pass

except Exception as e:

print(f"An error occurred: {e}")
```

3. Invalid Request Format:

- **Symptom:** The AI client sends a request, but the MCP server responds with an error indicating an invalid request format or missing parameters.

- **Possible Causes:**

  1. **Incorrect MCP Protocol Usage:** Your request might not adhere to the expected structure or naming conventions of the MCP protocol for the specific action you are trying to perform.
  2. **Missing Required Parameters:** The MCP server might be expecting certain parameters in the `context` of your request that are missing.
  3. **Incorrect Data Types:** The data you are sending in the request might not be in the expected format (e.g., sending a string when a number is expected).

- **Troubleshooting Steps:**

  1. **Consult MCP Protocol Documentation:** Carefully review the documentation for the specific MCP server and the API endpoints or actions you are using to ensure your requests are correctly formatted. Pay attention to required fields, data types, and the expected structure of the `context`.
  2. **Examine Server Error Messages:** The error message from the MCP server should provide clues about what is wrong with your request.
  3. **Validate Request Structure:** Print or log the request your AI client is sending to the server to visually inspect its format and content.

- **Conceptual Example (Python - ensuring request structure):**

- Python

```python
request = {

  "model_id": "my_ai_agent",

  "action": "retrieve_data",

  "context": {

    "data_source": "customer_orders",
```

```
        "query": "SELECT * FROM orders WHERE date
> '2024-01-01'"

        # Ensure all required fields are present and
correctly named

    }

}

response = mcp_client.send_request(request)
```

4. Data Format Issues (Response Parsing):

- **Symptom:** The MCP server returns a successful response, but your AI client fails to correctly parse or utilize the data in the response.

- **Possible Causes:**

    1. **Incorrect Assumption about Response Format:** You might be expecting the data in a different format than what the server is actually sending (e.g., expecting JSON but receiving CSV).
    2. **Unexpected Data Structure:** The structure of the data within the response might be different from what your client code is expecting.

3. **Errors in Client-Side Parsing Logic:** There might be bugs in your AI client's code that handles parsing the server's response.
- **Troubleshooting Steps:**

   1. **Inspect the Raw Response:** Print or log the raw response received from the MCP server to see its actual format and structure.
   2. **Verify Response Format (if specified in the request):** Ensure that the `response_format` you requested matches what the server is sending.
   3. **Consult MCP Protocol Documentation:** The documentation should describe the expected response format and data structure for different actions.
   4. **Debug Client-Side Parsing:** Carefully review the code in your AI client that handles parsing the server's response. Use debugging tools to step through the parsing logic and inspect the data.
- **Conceptual Example (Python - handling different response formats):**

- Python

```
response =
mcp_client.send_request(request_with_format_prefe
rence)
```

```python
if response.get("status") == "success":

    if
request_with_format_preference.get("response_form
at") == "json":

        data = response.get("data")

        # Process JSON data

    elif
request_with_format_preference.get("response_form
at") == "csv":

        data = response.get("data")

        # Process CSV data

    else:

        # Handle default format

        pass
```

5. Server Errors:

- **Symptom:** The AI client sends a valid request, but the MCP server returns an error indicating a problem on the server side (e.g., "Internal server error").
- **Possible Causes:**

1. **Bugs in the MCP Server Software:** The server itself might have a software defect.
2. **Resource Issues on the Server:** The server might be running out of memory, CPU, or disk space.
3. **Problems with Backend Services:** The MCP server might be unable to connect to a backend database or tool it relies on.
- **Troubleshooting Steps:**
    1. **Check Server Logs:** If you have access to the MCP server's logs, examine them for detailed error messages and stack traces that can provide clues about the issue.
    2. **Monitor Server Resources:** If you have access to server monitoring tools, check the CPU usage, memory usage, and disk space on the server machine.
    3. **Verify Backend Service Status:** If the error messages indicate issues with backend services, check the status and logs of those services.
    4. **Contact Server Administrators or Support:** If you are using a managed MCP server, contact the administrators or support team for assistance.
- **Personal Insight:** Server-side errors can be frustrating because they are often outside of your direct control as a client developer. Providing detailed information from the server logs to the support team is usually the most helpful step.

6.2 Simple Monitoring and Health Checks

Alright, let's talk about keeping an eye on things – simple monitoring and health checks for your MCP server and its interactions with AI. Think of this as regularly checking the pulse and vital signs of your intelligent system to ensure everything is running smoothly and identify potential issues early on.

Even for beginners, implementing basic monitoring and health checks can save a lot of headaches down the line. It allows you to proactively identify problems before they escalate and disrupt your AI-powered applications.

1. MCP Server Health Checks:

The first step is to ensure the MCP server itself is healthy and responsive. Many MCP server implementations provide built-in health check endpoints or mechanisms.

- **UI-Based Monitoring:**

    - **Dashboard Overview:** The server's dashboard often provides a high-level overview of its status, including indicators for CPU usage, memory usage, network activity, and the status of core services.[2] Keep an eye on any unusual spikes or persistent high utilization.
    - **Service Status:** Look for sections in the UI that list the status of individual components or services within

the MCP server (e.g., API gateway, data connectors, workflow engine). Ensure all critical services are reported as running and healthy.

- ○ **Log Monitoring:** Regularly review the server logs (accessible through the UI or log files) for any error messages or warnings. Pay attention to recurring issues.
- **API-Based Health Checks:**

  - ○ Many MCP servers expose a dedicated health check endpoint via their API (often at a simple URL like `/health` or `/status`). You can periodically query this endpoint to get a quick status report.

  - ○ **Conceptual Example (Python - checking a health endpoint):**

  - ○ Python

```python
import requests

import time


MCP_SERVER_URL = "http://your-mcp-server:8080"

HEALTH_CHECK_ENDPOINT = "/health"
```

```python
def check_server_health():

    try:

        response = requests.get(MCP_SERVER_URL +
HEALTH_CHECK_ENDPOINT)

        response.raise_for_status()  # Raise an exception for bad
status codes

        health_data = response.json()

        if health_data.get("status") == "ok":

            print(f"{time.ctime()}: MCP Server is healthy.")

            return True

        else:

            print(f"{time.ctime()}: MCP Server reports unhealthy status:
{health_data}")

            return False

    except requests.exceptions.RequestException as e:

        print(f"{time.ctime()}: Error checking server health: {e}")

        return False
```

```python
if __name__ == "__main__":

    while True:

        check_server_health()

        time.sleep(60)  # Check every minute
```

- **Explanation:** This simple Python script periodically sends a GET request to the `/health` endpoint of the MCP server. It checks the HTTP status code and the content of the JSON response for an "ok" status. Any errors or unhealthy status are printed.

2. Monitoring AI Interaction:

Beyond the server's health, you'll want to monitor the interactions between your AI clients and the MCP server.

- **Client-Side Logging:** Implement robust logging in your AI client applications to record all requests sent to the MCP server and the responses received. Include timestamps, request details, response status, and any error messages. This can be invaluable for debugging issues.

- Conceptual Example (Python - basic client-side logging):

- Python

```python
import logging

logging.basicConfig(level=logging.INFO, format='%(asctime)s - %(levelname)s - %(message)s')

class MyAiClient:
    def __init__(self, mcp_client):
        self.mcp_client = mcp_client

    def perform_task(self, data):
        request = {"model_id": "my_client", "action": "process_data", "context": {"input": data}}
        logging.info(f"Sending MCP Request: {request}")
        response = self.mcp_client.send_request(request)
        logging.info(f"Received MCP Response: {response}")
```

```
    return response
```

```
# ... (rest of the client code)
```

- **Server-Side Request/Response Logging:** The MCP
  server itself should log all incoming requests and outgoing
  responses. Reviewing these logs can help you understand
  the patterns of AI interaction, identify frequent errors, and
  monitor the performance of different actions.

- **Basic Performance Monitoring (Server-Side):** Keep an
  eye on basic performance metrics of the MCP server when
  AI models are actively interacting with it. High latency in
  responses or increased resource consumption during peak
  AI activity might indicate potential bottlenecks or the need
  for optimization.

3. Simple Alerting (Manual or Basic Automation):

While sophisticated monitoring systems with automated alerts are
ideal for production environments, even beginners can implement
simple forms of alerting:

- **Manual Checks with Notifications:** If you are regularly
  checking the server's UI or logs, set up simple reminders for
  yourself to do so. Some MCP servers might allow you to

configure basic email or other notifications for critical errors.[3]

- **Basic Scripted Checks:** You can extend the simple health check script from the API-based monitoring section to send an email or a message to a notification service (like Slack or a simple webhook) if the server is unhealthy.
  - **Conceptual Extension (Python - sending a basic alert):**

  - Python

```python
# (Import necessary libraries for sending emails or messages)


def check_server_health_with_alert():

    if not check_server_health():

        send_alert("MCP Server is unhealthy!")


def send_alert(message):

    print(f"ALERT: {message}")

    # (Code to send email, Slack message, etc.)


if __name__ == "__main__":
```

```
while True:

    check_server_health_with_alert()

    time.sleep(60)
```

Key Takeaways for Simple Monitoring:

- **Start Simple:** You don't need a complex monitoring system from day one. Focus on the basics: checking server health and logging client-server interactions.
- **Leverage Built-in Tools:** Explore the monitoring features provided by your MCP server's UI and API.
- **Log Everything Relevant:** Comprehensive logging on both the client and server sides is crucial for understanding and troubleshooting issues.
- **Be Proactive:** Regular checks can help you catch problems early before they cause significant disruptions.
- **Iterate and Improve:** As your system grows more complex, you can gradually introduce more sophisticated monitoring tools and alerting mechanisms.

6.3 Essential Maintenance Practices for Beginners

Alright, let's talk about keeping your MCP server environment in good shape. Think of essential maintenance practices as the regular upkeep you'd give a car or a home – it ensures everything runs smoothly, prevents bigger problems down the line, and extends the lifespan of your investment. For beginners, focusing on a few key areas will make a significant difference.

These practices will help you maintain a stable, secure, and performant MCP server environment for your AI interactions.

1. Regular Backups:

- **What it is:** Creating copies of your MCP server's configuration, data (if it stores any), and potentially even the entire server image.
- **Why it's essential:** In case of hardware failure, software corruption, accidental deletions, or security breaches, backups allow you to restore your system to a previous working state.
- **Beginner-Friendly Approach:**
    - **Identify Critical Data:** Determine what needs to be backed up. This usually includes configuration files, user databases (if any), and potentially logs.
    - **Manual Backups (Initial Stage):** Start by manually copying these critical files to a separate location (another hard drive, an external USB drive, or a secure cloud storage service).
    - **UI-Based Backup Tools (If Available):** Check if your MCP server's user interface offers any built-in backup or export functionality for configurations.
    - **Conceptual Example (Linux - manual backup):**
    - Bash

- # Assuming your MCP server configuration is in /etc/mcp/
- mkdir ~/mcp_backups
- cp -r /etc/mcp ~/mcp_backups/$(date +%Y%m%d_%H%M)
- # If you have a database, use database-specific backup tools (e.g., pg_dump for PostgreSQL)
- # pg_dump -U mcp_user mcp_database > ~/mcp_backups/mcp_db_$(date +%Y%m%d_%H%M).sql
-
- **Frequency:** Start with weekly backups. As your system becomes more critical, consider daily or even more frequent backups.
- **Personal Insight:** I once lost a significant amount of configuration data due to a hard drive failure. Since then, regular backups have become a non-negotiable part of my workflow.

2. Keeping Software Up-to-Date:

- **What it is:** Regularly updating your MCP server software, its dependencies (like operating system packages, programming language runtimes), and any related tools to the latest versions.
- **Why it's essential:** Updates often include bug fixes, performance improvements, and crucial security patches that protect your system from vulnerabilities.

- **Beginner-Friendly Approach:**
  - **Follow Release Notes:** Subscribe to the release announcements or check the official website of your MCP server to be aware of new versions.
  - **UI-Based Updates (If Available):** Many modern applications provide a straightforward way to update through their user interface. Look for "Updates" or "About" sections.
  - **Package Manager Updates (If Self-Hosted on Linux):** If you installed your MCP server using a package manager (like `apt` or `yum`), use those tools to update the server and the underlying system.
  - Bash
  - # Debian/Ubuntu:
  - sudo apt update
  - sudo apt upgrade <your_mcp_server_package_name>
  -
  - # CentOS/RHEL:
  - sudo yum update <your_mcp_server_package_name>
  -
  - **Docker Image Updates (If Using Docker):** If your MCP server runs in a Docker container, regularly pull the latest image from the official repository and redeploy your container.
  - Bash

- docker pull <your_mcp_server/image:latest>
- docker stop <your_container_name>
- docker rm <your_container_name>
- docker run -d --name <your_container_name> -p <ports> <your_mcp_server/image:latest> <other_options>
-
- **Caution:** Always read the release notes before updating, as major updates might introduce breaking changes. Consider testing updates in a non-production environment first if possible.

3. Monitoring Resource Usage:

- **What it is:** Regularly checking the CPU utilization, memory usage, disk space, and network activity of your MCP server.
- **Why it's essential:** Identifying unusual spikes or consistently high resource usage can indicate performance bottlenecks, potential issues, or the need for scaling your infrastructure.
- **Beginner-Friendly Approach:**
  - **Operating System Monitoring Tools:** Use built-in tools like Task Manager (Windows) or top/htop (Linux) to get a real-time view of resource consumption.
  - **MCP Server Dashboard:** The server's UI often provides graphs and charts showing resource utilization.

- ○ **Basic Scripted Monitoring:** You can write simple scripts to periodically check resource usage and alert you if thresholds are exceeded (as discussed in the previous section on monitoring).
- **Personal Insight:** I've used resource monitoring to identify runaway processes consuming excessive CPU and memory, allowing me to address the issue before it caused a system crash.

4. Log Management:

- **What it is:** Regularly reviewing, archiving, and potentially rotating your MCP server's logs.
- **Why it's essential:** Logs contain valuable information for troubleshooting errors, understanding system behavior, and auditing security events. However, they can also consume significant disk space over time.
- **Beginner-Friendly Approach:**
  - ○ **Regular Review:** Periodically glance through the server logs for any recurring errors or warnings.
  - ○ **Log Archiving:** Consider moving older log files to a separate directory or storage to prevent them from filling up your main disk.
  - ○ **Log Rotation (If Available):** Many systems have built-in log rotation mechanisms that automatically archive old logs and delete the oldest ones based on defined rules. Check your MCP server's configuration for log rotation settings.

- **Conceptual Example (Linux - basic log archiving):**
- Bash
- mkdir ~/mcp_logs_archive
- mv /var/log/mcp_server/*.log.1 ~/mcp_logs_archive/$(date +%Y%m%d)
- # .1 usually indicates rotated log files

5. Security Awareness:

- **What it is:** Staying informed about potential security vulnerabilities and following basic security best practices.
- **Why it's essential:** Protecting your MCP server and the data it handles is paramount, especially when AI models are involved.
- **Beginner-Friendly Approach:**
  - **Strong Passwords:** Use strong, unique passwords for all accounts associated with your MCP server.
  - **Principle of Least Privilege:** Grant only the necessary permissions to users and AI clients.
  - **Firewall Configuration:** Ensure your firewall is properly configured to allow only necessary traffic to your MCP server.
  - **Stay Informed:** Follow security advisories related to your MCP server software and its dependencies.
  - **Regular Updates (Reiterated):** Keeping your software up-to-date is a crucial security measure.

Getting Started with Maintenance:

Don't feel overwhelmed by this list. Start with the most critical practices: **regular backups and keeping your software updated.** Then, gradually incorporate resource monitoring and log management into your routine. Security should always be a consideration from the beginning.

By adopting these essential maintenance practices, even as a beginner, you'll be well-equipped to maintain a healthy and reliable MCP server environment, ensuring smoother interactions with your AI applications and preventing potential disruptions.

6.4 Basic Security Tips for New Users

Alright, let's talk about something super important: keeping your MCP server and everything connected to it secure. Think of these basic security tips as locking your doors and windows – they're fundamental steps that significantly reduce your risk. Even if you're just starting out, implementing these practices will create a much safer environment for your intelligent applications.

Security isn't just for experts; it's a responsibility for everyone who manages or interacts with an MCP server. Here are some essential tips to get you started on the right foot:

1. Strong and Unique Passwords:

- **What it is:** Using complex passwords that are difficult to guess and are unique to each account (your MCP server login, database credentials, etc.).
- **Why it's essential:** Weak or reused passwords are the easiest way for attackers to gain unauthorized access.
- **Beginner-Friendly Approach:**
  - **Length Matters:** Aim for passwords that are at least 12 characters long. Longer is generally better.
  - **Mix It Up:** Include a combination of uppercase and lowercase letters, numbers, and symbols (!@#$%^&*).
  - **Avoid Personal Information:** Don't use easily guessable information like your name, birthday, pet's name, or common words.
  - **Use a Password Manager:** Consider using a reputable password manager to generate and securely store strong, unique passwords for all your accounts. This way, you only need to remember one strong master password.
  - **Never Share Passwords:** Keep your passwords confidential and avoid writing them down in easily accessible places.
- **Conceptual Example (Illustrating weak vs. strong password):**
  - **Weak:** `password123`, `mcp_server`, `mybirthday`

- **Strong:** `P@$$w0rd!2025`, `gHu7#jKl9*zXy`, `Lmn$Opq^RsT&UvW`

2. Enable Multi-Factor Authentication (MFA):

- **What it is:** Adding an extra layer of security beyond just a password. Typically, this involves providing a second verification factor, such as a code from your phone (via an authenticator app or SMS), a fingerprint, or a security key.
- **Why it's essential:** Even if your password is compromised, MFA makes it much harder for an attacker to gain access without also having your second factor.
- **Beginner-Friendly Approach:**
    1. **Check Server Settings:** See if your MCP server offers MFA options in its security or user profile settings.
    2. **Authenticator Apps:** Apps like Google Authenticator, Authy, or Microsoft Authenticator are easy to set up and provide time-based one-time passwords (TOTP).
    3. **SMS Verification:** While less secure than authenticator apps, SMS-based MFA is better than no MFA at all.
    4. **Enable for All Accounts:** Enable MFA for your MCP server login and any related services (like the underlying operating system or database).

- **Conceptual Example (Illustrating MFA flow):**
    1. You enter your username and password to log in to the MCP server.
    2. The server prompts you for a second verification factor.
    3. You open your authenticator app on your phone and enter the time-sensitive code displayed.
    4. Only after providing the correct code are you granted access.

3. Firewall Configuration:

- **What it is:** Controlling the network traffic that can reach your MCP server by specifying which ports and IP addresses are allowed to connect.
- **Why it's essential:** A properly configured firewall prevents unauthorized access to your server from the internet or other networks.
- **Beginner-Friendly Approach:**
    - **Identify Necessary Ports:** Determine which network ports your MCP server needs to be accessible on (e.g., the HTTP/HTTPS port for the UI, any API ports). The default port is often documented.
    - **Restrict Access:** Configure your firewall (whether it's built into your operating system or a dedicated hardware firewall) to allow connections only on these necessary ports and ideally only from trusted IP addresses if possible.

- Disable Unnecessary Services: Turn off any network services running on your server that you don't need.
- Conceptual Example (Basic Firewall Rule - allowing HTTP on port 80):
- Bash

```
# Linux (using UFW - Uncomplicated Firewall)

sudo ufw allow 80/tcp

sudo ufw enable

sudo ufw status
```

- Note: Firewall configuration can vary depending on your operating system and network setup. Consult the documentation for your specific environment.

4. Principle of Least Privilege:

- **What it is:** Granting users, AI models, and applications only the minimum level of access and permissions they need to perform their specific tasks.
- **Why it's essential:** Limiting privileges reduces the potential damage if an account is compromised. An attacker with limited access can't do as much harm.
- **Beginner-Friendly Approach:**

- **Separate User Accounts:** Create separate user accounts for different individuals or AI agents, each with only the necessary permissions. Avoid using the root or administrator account for everyday tasks.
- **Role-Based Access Control (RBAC):** If your MCP server supports RBAC, define roles with specific sets of permissions (e.g., "Data Reader," "Workflow Executor") and assign these roles to users or AI agents based on their responsibilities.
- **API Key Scopes:** If your AI models interact with the MCP server via API keys, ensure these keys have limited scopes, granting access only to the specific actions and resources the AI needs.

- **Conceptual Example (Illustrating RBAC):**
  - An AI model responsible for retrieving product information is granted the "Data Reader" role, allowing it to query the product database but not modify it.
  - A user responsible for managing workflows is granted the "Workflow Editor" role, allowing them to create, edit, and trigger workflows but not manage user accounts.

5. Keep Software Updated (Reiterated for Security):

- **Why it's essential (Security Focus):** Software updates frequently include patches for known security vulnerabilities.

Running outdated software exposes your system to these risks.

- **Beginner-Friendly Approach:**
  - **Enable Automatic Updates (with caution):** Some systems offer automatic updates. While convenient, consider configuring them to notify you before installing, so you can review the changes.
  - **Regular Manual Checks:** Make it a habit to check for updates for your MCP server, operating system, and any related software on a regular basis.
  - **Apply Security Patches Promptly:** Prioritize installing security updates as soon as they are released.

6. Secure Your Communication (HTTPS):

- **What it is:** Encrypting the communication between your web browser and the MCP server's user interface using HTTPS (Hypertext Transfer Protocol Secure).
- **Why it's essential:** HTTPS prevents eavesdropping and ensures that sensitive information (like login credentials) is transmitted securely.
- **Beginner-Friendly Approach:**
  - **Check for HTTPS:** When accessing the MCP server's UI in your browser, look for "https://" at the beginning of the URL and a padlock icon in the address bar.

- **Configure HTTPS (If Not Enabled by Default):** If your server isn't using HTTPS, consult its documentation on how to enable it. This usually involves obtaining and configuring an SSL/TLS certificate. Let's Encrypt provides free and easy-to-use certificates.

Getting Started with Security:

Don't try to implement all of these tips at once. Start with the most fundamental ones: **strong passwords, enabling MFA, and configuring a basic firewall.** Then, gradually work your way through the other recommendations. Security is an ongoing process, so stay informed and be proactive. Your efforts in implementing these basic security measures will go a long way in protecting your intelligent MCP server environment.

Chapter 7: Further Learning and Next Steps

The world of technology is constantly evolving, and MCP servers are no exception. This chapter will provide you with valuable resources to deepen your understanding and continue to grow your skills. We'll also touch upon some more advanced topics that you might want to explore as you become more comfortable.

7.1 Where to Find Additional Resources and Support

Alright, as you continue your journey with MCP servers and AI orchestration, you'll inevitably have more questions and might need some help along the way. Think of this section as your compass and map to navigate the landscape of additional resources and support. Knowing where to turn when you're stuck or want to learn more is crucial for your growth and success.

Here's a guide to the various places where you can find more information, get help with specific issues, and connect with the community around MCP servers and related technologies.

1. Official Documentation:

- **What it is:** The primary source of information provided by the creators or maintainers of your specific MCP server software.
- **Why it's invaluable:** It contains the most accurate and up-to-date details about installation, configuration, usage, API references, troubleshooting guides, and best practices.
- **Beginner-Friendly Approach:**
  - **Locate the Documentation:** The documentation is usually found on the official website of the MCP server project. Look for sections like "Docs," "Documentation," "Manual," or "Guide."
  - **Start with the Basics:** Begin with introductory guides and tutorials to get a solid foundation.
  - **Use the Search Function:** Most documentation sites have a search bar to quickly find information on specific topics or keywords.
  - **Pay Attention to Examples:** Look for code snippets, configuration examples, and step-by-step instructions.
  - **Check the FAQ:** The Frequently Asked Questions (FAQ) section often addresses common beginner issues.
- **Personal Insight:** I've often found that a thorough read of the official documentation, even when I think I know the basics, reveals nuances and features I wasn't aware of.

2. Community Forums and Discussion Boards:

- **What they are:** Online platforms where users of a specific software or technology can ask questions, share knowledge, discuss use cases, and help each other troubleshoot problems.
- **Why they're helpful:** You can connect with other learners and experienced users, find solutions to common issues, and get diverse perspectives.
- **Beginner-Friendly Approach:**
  - **Find the Official Forum:** Many MCP server projects have their own community forums hosted on their website or platforms like Discourse or similar.
  - **Look for Relevant Subreddits or Groups:** Platforms like Reddit (subreddits related to AI, machine learning, or specific technologies used by the MCP server) and other online communities (e.g., on platforms like Slack or Discord) can be valuable.
  - **Search Before Asking:** Before posting a new question, search the forum archives to see if your issue has already been discussed.
  - **Be Clear and Concise:** When asking a question, provide as much relevant information as possible (e.g., your setup, the specific error messages you're seeing, what you've already tried).
  - **Be Patient and Respectful:** Remember that community members are volunteers helping in their free time. Be polite and patient in your interactions.

3. Online Courses and Tutorials:

- **What they are:** Structured learning materials available on platforms like Coursera, edX, Udemy, YouTube, and the MCP server's official website.
- **Why they're beneficial:** They offer a guided learning experience, often with video lectures, hands-on exercises, and quizzes to reinforce your understanding.
- **Beginner-Friendly Approach:**
  - **Start with Introductory Courses:** Look for courses specifically designed for beginners in AI orchestration or the specific technologies used by your MCP server.
  - **Follow Step-by-Step Tutorials:** Many websites and YouTube channels offer tutorials that walk you through specific tasks or concepts.
  - **Practice the Examples:** Don't just watch or read; actively try out the code examples and exercises provided.
  - **Look for Courses with Active Communities:** Some online learning platforms have forums or discussion groups associated with their courses where you can ask questions.

4. Example Projects and Repositories:

- **What they are:** Open-source projects and code repositories (often on platforms like GitHub) that demonstrate how to use MCP servers and integrate them with AI models and other systems.

- **Why they're useful:** You can learn by example, see how experienced developers structure their projects, and potentially reuse or adapt existing code.

- **Beginner-Friendly Approach:**
  - **Search on GitHub:** Use keywords related to your MCP server and the types of AI interactions you're interested in (e.g., "MCP server Python example," "MCP server workflow").
  - **Look for Well-Documented Projects:** Choose repositories with clear README files, setup instructions, and example code.
  - **Start with Simple Examples:** Begin by understanding basic examples before tackling more complex projects.
  - **Contribute (Once Comfortable):** As you gain experience, consider contributing back to the community by sharing your own examples or improvements.

5. Vendor Support (If Applicable):

- **What it is:** Direct support provided by the company or organization that develops and maintains the MCP server software (especially for commercial versions).

- **Why it's important:** For paid versions, you often get access to dedicated support channels, service level agreements (SLAs), and expert assistance.
- **Beginner-Friendly Approach:**
  - **Check Support Options:** Explore the support resources offered by the vendor, such as email support, ticketing systems, phone support, or knowledge bases.
  - **Provide Detailed Information:** When contacting support, be as specific as possible about your issue, including error messages, configuration details, and the steps you've already taken.

6. Local Meetups and Conferences:

- **What they are:** In-person or virtual events where you can connect with other professionals and enthusiasts in the AI and related fields.
- **Why they're valuable:** Networking with others can lead to learning opportunities, problem-solving, and staying up-to-date with the latest trends.
- **Beginner-Friendly Approach:**
  - **Search for Local Groups:** Look for meetups related to AI, machine learning, cloud computing, or specific technologies relevant to your MCP server in your area (or online). Platforms like Meetup.com can be helpful.

- ○ **Attend Beginner-Friendly Sessions:** Many events have sessions specifically targeted at newcomers.
- ○ **Don't Be Afraid to Ask Questions:** Meetups are great places to connect with experienced individuals and ask for advice.

Key to Effective Resource Utilization:

- **Be Specific:** When seeking help, clearly articulate your problem and what you've already tried.
- **Be Patient:** Solutions might not always be immediate.
- **Be Respectful:** Engage constructively with community members and support staff.
- **Give Back:** Once you gain experience, consider contributing to the community by answering questions or sharing your knowledge.

7.2 Suggestions for Continued Learning and Skill Development

Alright, you've taken the first steps into the world of MCP servers and AI interaction – that's fantastic! But the landscape of AI and orchestration is constantly evolving, so continuous learning is key to staying relevant and maximizing your potential. Think of this section as your roadmap for expanding your skills and deepening your understanding.

Here are some actionable suggestions to help you on your journey of continuous learning and skill development in the realm of MCP servers and AI orchestration:

1. Deep Dive into Your Specific MCP Server:

- **Action:** Go beyond the basics of the MCP server you are currently using. Explore its advanced features, configuration options, and API capabilities in detail.
- **Why it's important:** Each MCP server has its own strengths and unique functionalities. Mastering your primary toolset will make you more effective.
- **Beginner-Friendly Approach:**
  - **Advanced Documentation:** Read the sections of the official documentation that cover more advanced topics like security configurations, scaling strategies, custom extensions, and integration with specific AI platforms or tools.
  - **Advanced Tutorials and Workshops:** Look for tutorials or workshops provided by the MCP server vendor or community that focus on specific advanced use cases.
  - **Experiment with Features:** Don't be afraid to try out different configuration options and features in a non-production environment to see how they work.
  - **Contribute to the Project (If Open Source):** If your MCP server is open source, consider contributing to the documentation, reporting bugs, or even

submitting code changes as you become more proficient.

2. Broaden Your Understanding of Underlying Technologies:

- **Action:** Expand your knowledge of the core technologies that often underpin MCP servers and AI interactions.
- **Why it's important:** A solid understanding of these foundations will give you a deeper insight into how things work and enable you to troubleshoot more effectively.
- **Beginner-Friendly Approach:**
    - **Networking Fundamentals:** Learn about TCP/IP, HTTP/HTTPS, DNS, and basic network security concepts.
    - **Cloud Computing Basics:** Familiarize yourself with concepts from major cloud providers (AWS, Azure, GCP) if your MCP server or AI models are cloud-based. Understand services like compute instances, storage, and basic networking.
    - **Containerization (Docker, Kubernetes):** If your MCP server uses containers, learn the basics of Docker for managing individual containers and Kubernetes for orchestrating them at scale. Numerous beginner-friendly tutorials are available online.
    - **API Concepts (REST, gRPC):** Understand how APIs work, the principles of RESTful APIs (common in

web services), and potentially explore gRPC for high-performance communication.

- **Data Formats (JSON, YAML):** Become comfortable working with common data serialization formats like JSON and YAML, as they are frequently used in configuration and API communication.

3. Enhance Your Programming Skills:

- **Action:** If you're interacting with the MCP server programmatically (e.g., using an SDK), continue to improve your programming skills in the relevant language (often Python, Java, or Node.js).
- **Why it's important:** Strong programming skills will allow you to build more sophisticated AI integrations and automation workflows.
- **Beginner-Friendly Approach:**
  - **Online Courses:** Take intermediate and advanced courses in your chosen programming language, focusing on areas relevant to API interaction, data handling, and asynchronous programming.
  - **Practice Regularly:** Work on small projects that involve interacting with the MCP server's API.
  - **Explore Libraries and Frameworks:** Familiarize yourself with libraries that simplify API calls, data parsing, and other common tasks.
  - **Learn About Software Design Principles:** Understanding concepts like modularity, reusability,

and error handling will help you write more robust code.

4. Dive Deeper into AI and Machine Learning:

- **Action:** Expand your knowledge of AI and machine learning concepts beyond just using pre-trained models.
- **Why it's important:** Understanding the fundamentals of AI will help you make more informed decisions about how to leverage AI models through your MCP server.
- **Beginner-Friendly Approach:**
  - **Introductory ML Courses:** Take courses that cover the basics of different types of machine learning (supervised, unsupervised, reinforcement learning), common algorithms, and model evaluation.
  - **Explore Specific AI Domains:** Focus on areas relevant to your use cases (e.g., Natural Language Processing, Computer Vision, Time Series Analysis).
  - **Learn About Model Deployment and Management:** Understand the challenges and best practices involved in deploying and monitoring AI models in production, as this is a key function of many MCP servers.

5. Explore Related Ecosystems and Tools:

- **Action:** Investigate tools and platforms that often integrate with MCP servers, such as AI model registries (MLflow), data science platforms (Jupyter, Colab), and workflow orchestration tools (Airflow, Prefect).

- **Why it's important:** Understanding these related tools can help you build more comprehensive and powerful intelligent systems.
- **Beginner-Friendly Approach:**
  - **Introduction Tutorials:** Look for introductory tutorials on how these tools work and how they can be integrated with MCP servers.
  - **Community Integrations:** Explore any community-developed integrations or examples that show how different tools can be used together.
  - **Focus on Your Needs:** Don't try to learn everything at once. Focus on the tools that are most relevant to your current or near-future projects.

6. Engage with the Community (Actively):

- **Action:** Go beyond just reading forums and actively participate by asking and answering questions, sharing your experiences, and contributing to discussions.
- **Why it's important:** Engaging with the community is a great way to learn from others, get different perspectives, and build your professional network.
- **Beginner-Friendly Approach:**
  - **Answer Questions (If You Can):** Even if you're a beginner, you might have insights that can help others.

- **Share Your Learnings:** Write blog posts, create tutorials, or share code examples of things you've learned.
- **Participate in Discussions:** Offer your thoughts and perspectives on relevant topics.

7. Build Practical Projects:

- **Action:** Apply your knowledge by working on real-world (or realistic) projects that involve using an MCP server to orchestrate AI interactions.
- **Why it's important:** Practical experience is the best way to solidify your learning and develop valuable skills.
- **Beginner-Friendly Approach:**
  - **Start Small:** Begin with simple projects that focus on one or two key concepts.
  - **Follow Project-Based Tutorials:** Many online resources offer project-based learning experiences.
  - **Contribute to Open Source Projects:** Working on existing projects can provide valuable hands-on experience.
  - **Document Your Work:** Clearly document your projects, including your goals, the steps you took, and any challenges you faced.

Key to Continued Growth:

- **Be Curious:** Cultivate a curious mindset and always be eager to learn new things.

- **Be Persistent:** Learning complex technologies takes time and effort. Don't get discouraged by challenges.
- **Be Patient:** Progress might not always be linear. Celebrate your small wins and keep moving forward.

7.3 Exploring More Advanced MCP Server Concepts: Unleashing the Full Potential

These concepts often involve more complex configurations, deeper integrations, and strategies for handling larger and more demanding AI orchestration tasks. While providing complete, working code examples for each advanced concept can be intricate and highly dependent on the specific MCP server, I'll provide conceptual explanations and highlight key considerations.

1. Scalability and High Availability:

- **What it is:** Designing your MCP server infrastructure to handle increasing workloads (scalability) and ensuring continuous operation even if individual components fail (high availability).
- **Why it's important:** For production environments and critical AI applications, scalability and high availability are paramount to maintain performance and prevent service disruptions.
- **Advanced Considerations:**
    - **Horizontal Scaling:** Adding more instances of your MCP server to distribute the load. This often involves

load balancers to direct traffic and shared storage or a distributed data store for state management.

- ○ **Vertical Scaling:** Increasing the resources (CPU, RAM, storage) of individual MCP server instances.
- ○ **Replication and Clustering:** Configuring multiple MCP server instances to work together, often with automatic failover mechanisms.
- ○ **Stateless Design:** Designing your AI interaction workflows to minimize reliance on the state of individual server instances, making horizontal scaling easier.
- ○ **Load Balancing Algorithms:** Understanding different load balancing strategies (e.g., round robin, least connections) and choosing the one that best suits your workload.
- **Conceptual Illustration:** Imagine your AI-powered customer service chatbot suddenly experiences a massive surge in users during a flash sale. A scalable MCP server architecture would automatically spin up more instances to handle the increased load without performance degradation. If one of the server instances fails, the load balancer would direct traffic to the remaining healthy instances, ensuring continuous service.

2. Advanced Workflow Orchestration:

- **What it is:** Designing and managing complex, multi-step workflows involving various AI models, tools, data sources, and conditional logic.
- **Why it's important:** Real-world AI applications often require intricate sequences of actions. Advanced orchestration allows you to define and manage these complex processes.
- **Advanced Considerations:**
  - **Directed Acyclic Graphs (DAGs):** Representing workflows as DAGs to define dependencies and execution order.
  - **Conditional Branching:** Implementing logic that allows different paths to be taken in a workflow based on the outcome of previous steps.
  - **Parallel Execution:** Running independent steps of a workflow concurrently to improve efficiency.
  - **Error Handling and Retries:** Implementing robust mechanisms to handle failures within a workflow, including retrying failed steps or executing alternative actions.
  - **State Management:** Tracking the progress and data associated with running workflow instances.
  - **Workflow Versioning and Management:** Handling updates and changes to workflows over time.
- **Conceptual Illustration:** An AI-driven content creation pipeline might involve a workflow with steps like: 1. Receive

user input. 2. Generate initial draft using a language model. 3. Perform fact-checking using a knowledge retrieval tool. 4. Edit and refine the draft with human-in-the-loop intervention. 5. Generate images using an image generation model. 6. Publish the final content. Advanced orchestration allows you to define this entire process, handle potential errors at each step, and manage different versions of the workflow.

3. Custom Integrations and Extensions:

- **What it is:** Extending the functionality of the MCP server by integrating with custom tools, AI models, or external systems that are not natively supported.
- **Why it's important:** Allows you to tailor the MCP server to your specific needs and leverage specialized AI capabilities or existing infrastructure.
- **Advanced Considerations:**
  - **Plugin Architectures:** Many MCP servers provide plugin or extension mechanisms to add custom functionality.
  - **API Development:** Building custom APIs that the MCP server can interact with to access external resources or trigger custom logic.
  - **Custom Task/Action Development:** Defining new types of tasks or actions that can be used within automation workflows.

- **Data Transformation and Mapping:** Implementing custom logic to transform data between different formats or schemas during integrations.
- **Security Considerations for Custom Code:** Ensuring that any custom integrations are developed with security best practices in mind.
- **Conceptual Illustration:** You might have a proprietary AI model trained for a very specific task. An advanced MCP server would allow you to build a custom integration (e.g., a plugin or a custom API endpoint) that the MCP server can use to send data to your model and receive predictions as part of an automated workflow.

4. Advanced Security Measures:

- **What it is:** Implementing more sophisticated security practices beyond the basics, especially in production environments.
- **Why it's important:** Protecting sensitive data, preventing unauthorized access, and ensuring the integrity of your AI systems are critical.
- **Advanced Considerations:**
    - **Network Segmentation:** Isolating your MCP server and related components within your network to limit the impact of a security breach.
    - **Intrusion Detection and Prevention Systems (IDPS):** Implementing tools to monitor network traffic for malicious activity.

- Regular Security Audits and Penetration Testing: Periodically assessing your system for vulnerabilities.
- Secure Credential Management: Using secure methods for storing and managing API keys, tokens, and other sensitive credentials (e.g., using secrets management tools like HashiCorp Vault).
- Data Encryption at Rest and in Transit: Encrypting sensitive data stored on the server and during communication.
- Advanced Authentication and Authorization (e.g., OAuth 2.0, SAML): Implementing more robust authentication and authorization mechanisms for users and AI clients.

5. Monitoring and Observability at Scale:

- **What it is:** Implementing comprehensive monitoring and observability solutions to gain deep insights into the performance, health, and behavior of your[1] MCP server and its managed AI interactions at scale.
- **Why it's important:** Essential for identifying performance bottlenecks, troubleshooting complex issues, and understanding the overall health of your distributed intelligent system.
- **Advanced Considerations:**
  - **Centralized Logging:** Aggregating logs from all MCP server instances and related components into a central system for easier analysis.

- **Metrics Collection and Visualization:** Collecting key performance indicators (KPIs) like request latency, error rates, resource utilization, and visualizing them using tools like Grafana or Kibana.
- **Distributed Tracing:** Tracking the flow of requests across multiple services to identify performance bottlenecks and understand dependencies.
- **Alerting and Anomaly Detection:** Setting up sophisticated alerting rules based on various metrics and potentially using anomaly detection techniques to proactively identify issues.

Moving Towards Mastery:

Exploring these advanced concepts will significantly enhance your ability to build and manage robust, scalable, and secure AI orchestration platforms using MCP servers. Remember that the specific implementation details will vary depending on the MCP server you are using. The key is to:

- **Consult the Advanced Documentation:** This will be your primary guide.
- **Experiment in Non-Production Environments:** Don't make changes to production systems without thorough testing.
- **Learn from Case Studies and Best Practices:** See how others are implementing these advanced concepts.

- **Continuously Learn and Adapt:** The field of AI orchestration is constantly evolving, so stay curious and keep learning.